Praise for *The Great Degeneration*

"[Ferguson's] intellectual virtuosity is refreshing. *The Great Degeneration* won't be popular in the Obama White House or other centers of power. Jeremiah wasn't popular with the elders of Judea either. They tossed him in jail for his sedition. They had reason later to be sorry."
—*The Wall Street Journal*

"Unlike most historians the author is capable of understanding the technical literature and explaining its conclusions in straightforward terms. . . . An informative and enjoyable read." —*Financial Times*

"[Ferguson] delivers an entertaining, often convincing polemic." —*Kirkus Reviews*

"Succinct and insightful . . . He provides not only a perceptive analysis of our society's past successes, but also a sobering diagnosis of our present and future. . . . This is a powerful and persuasive book." —*The Washington Times*

"Concise and important . . . The economy is as delicate and self-perpetuating as an ecosystem, Ferguson brilliantly argues, the most complex creation man has ever managed." —*Toronto Star*

"Historians often get it wrong when they turn to the present and the future, but *Degeneration*, based on the author's Reith Lectures, is a compelling and cogently argued work."
—*Times Higher Education* (London)

"Ferguson frames the problems of our time with the simplicity that is the hallmark of a powerful mind."
—History News Network

PENGUIN BOOKS

THE GREAT DEGENERATION

Niall Ferguson is one of the world's most renowned historians. He is the author of sixteen books, including *Civilization*; *Doom*; *The Square and the Tower*; *Kissinger, 1923–1968: The Idealist*; and *The Ascent of Money*. He is the Milbank Family Senior Fellow at the Hoover Institution, Stanford University, and the managing director of Greenmantle LLC. His many awards include the Benjamin Franklin Prize for Public Service (2010), the Hayek Prize for Lifetime Achievement (2012) and the Ludwig Erhard Prize for Economic Journalism (2013).

niallferguson.com

The Great Degeneration

How Institutions Decay and Economies Die

NIALL FERGUSON

PENGUIN BOOKS

PENGUIN BOOKS
Published by the Penguin Group
Penguin Group (USA) LLC
375 Hudson Street
New York, New York 10014

USA | Canada | UK | Ireland | Australia | New Zealand | India | South Africa | China
penguin.com
A Penguin Random House Company

First published in Great Britain by Allen Lane, an imprint of Penguin Books Ltd. 2012
First published in the United States of America by Viking Penguin,
a member of Penguin Group (USA) Inc., 2013
Published in Penguin Books 2014

THE LIBRARY OF CONGRESS HAS CATALOGED THE HARDCOVER EDITION AS FOLLOWS:

Ferguson, Niall.
The great degeneration : how institutions decay and economies die / Niall Ferguson.
pages   cm
Includes bibliographical references.
ISBN 978-1-59420-545-3 (hc.)
ISBN 978-0-14-312552-5 (pbk.)
1. Developed countries—Social conditions—21st century.   2. Developed countries—
Economic conditions—21st century.   3. Social institutions—Developed countries.
4. Civil society—Developed countries.   5. Civilization, Western—21st century.
6. Regression (Civilization)   I. Title.
HN19.F47   2013
306.09172'4—dc23
2012046983

for
Thomas

Contents

List of Figures

The Great Degeneration

Introduction

Beyond 'Deleveraging'

Almost a quarter of a century ago, in the summer of 1989, Francis Fukuyama could boldly predict 'an unabashed victory of economic and political liberalism . . . the Triumph of the West' and proclaim that 'the end point of mankind's ideological evolution' was 'the universalization of Western liberal democracy as the final form of human government'.[1] How different the world looks now. 'Economic liberalism' is a tarnished brand, while the proponents of 'state capitalism' in China and elsewhere openly deride Western democracy. The West is stagnating, and not only in economic terms. In 2013 the World Bank expected the European economy to contract and the US to grow by just 1.6 per cent. China would grow four times faster than that, India two and a half times faster. By 2018, according to the International Monetary Fund, the gross domestic product of China would approach that of the United States.* Those who invested in the West in 1989 have been punished (they have made nothing since 2000), while those who invested in the Rest have been richly rewarded. This 'great reconvergence' is a far more astonishing historical event than the collapse of communism that Fukuyama so astutely anticipated. At the time he wrote, the world's centre of economic gravity was still firmly in the North Atlantic. Today it is beyond the Urals, and by 2025 it will be just north of Kazakhstan – on roughly the same line of latitude as it was in 1500, on the eve of Western ascendancy.[2]

The voguish explanation for the Western slowdown is 'deleveraging': the painful process of debt reduction (or balance sheet repair). Certainly, there are few precedents for the scale of debt in the West today. This is only the second time in American history that combined public and private debt has exceeded 250 per cent of GDP. In a survey of fifty countries, the McKinsey Global Institute identifies forty-five episodes of deleveraging since 1930. In only eight was the initial debt/GDP ratio above 250 per cent, as it is today not only in the US but also in all the major English-speaking countries (including Australia and Canada), all the major continental European countries (including Germany), plus Japan and South Korea.[3] The

---

* On a purchasing-power parity basis, adjusting for the fact that non-tradable goods and services are much cheaper in China than in the United States. In current dollar terms, the Chinese economy will still be 60 per cent the size of the American in 2016 – compared with just 8 per cent in 1989.

deleveraging argument is that households and banks are struggling to reduce their debts, having gambled foolishly on ever rising property prices. But as people have sought to spend less and save more, aggregate demand has slumped. To prevent this process from generating a lethal debt deflation, governments and central banks have stepped in with fiscal and monetary stimulus unparalleled in time of peace. Public sector deficits have helped to mitigate the contraction, but they risk transforming a crisis of excess private debt into a crisis of excess public debt. In the same way, the expansion of central bank balance sheets (the monetary base) prevented a cascade of bank failures, but now appears to have diminishing returns in terms of reflation and growth.

Yet more is going on here than just deleveraging. Consider this: the US economy created 2.4 million jobs in the three years beginning in June 2009. In the same period, 3.3 million Americans were awarded disabled worker benefits. The percentage of working-age Americans collecting disability insurance has risen from below 3 per cent in 1990 to 6 per cent.[4] Unemployment is being concealed – and rendered permanent – in ways all too familiar to Europeans. Able-bodied people are classified as disabled and never work again. And they also stay put. Traditionally around 3 per cent of the US population moves to a new state each year, usually in pursuit of work. That rate has halved since the financial crisis began in 2007. Social mobility has also declined. And, unlike the Great Depression of the 1930s, our 'Slight Depression' is doing little to reduce the yawning inequality in income distribution that has developed over the past three decades. The income share of the top 1 per cent of households rose from 9 per cent in 1970 to 24 per cent in 2007. It declined by less than 4 percentage points in the subsequent three years of crisis.

You cannot blame all this on deleveraging. In the United States, the wider debate is about globalization, technological change, education and fiscal policy. Conservatives tend to emphasize the first and second as inexorable drivers of change, destroying low-skilled jobs by 'offshoring' or automating them. Liberals prefer to see widening inequality as the result of insufficient investment in public education, combined with Republican reductions in taxation that have favoured the wealthy.[5] But there is good reason to think that there are other forces at work – forces that tend to get overlooked in the slanging match that passes for political debate in the United States today.

The crisis of public finance is not uniquely American. Japan, Greece, Italy, Ireland and Portugal are also members of the club of countries with public debts in excess of 100 per cent of GDP. India had an even larger cyclically adjusted deficit than the United States in 2010, while Japan faced a bigger challenge to stabilize its debt/GDP ratio at a sustainable level.[6] Nor are the twin problems of slow growth and widening inequality confined to the United States. Throughout the English-speaking world, the income share of the top '1 per cent' of households has risen since around 1980. The same thing has happened, albeit to a lesser extent, in some European states, notably Finland, Norway and Portugal, as well as in many emerging markets, including China.[7] Already in 2010 there were at least 800,000 dollar millionaires in China and sixty-five billionaires. Of the global '1 per cent' in 2010, 1.6 million were Chinese, approaching 4 per cent of the total.[8] Yet other countries, including Europe's most successful economy, Germany, have not become more unequal, while some less developed countries, notably Argentina, have become less equal without becoming more global.

By definition, globalization has affected all countries to some degree. So, too, has the revolution in information technology. Yet the outcomes in terms of growth and distribution vary hugely. To explain these differences, a narrowly economic approach is not sufficient. Take the case of excessive debt or leverage. Any highly indebted economy confronts a narrow range of options. There are essentially three:

1. raising the rate of growth above the rate of interest thanks to technological innovation and (perhaps) a judicious use of monetary stimulus;
2. defaulting on a large proportion of the public debt and going into bankruptcy to escape the private debt; and
3. wiping out of debts via currency depreciation and inflation.

But nothing in mainstream economic theory can predict which of these three – or which combination – a particular country will select. Why did post-1918 Germany go down the road of hyperinflation? Why did post-1929 America go down the road of private default and bankruptcy? Why not the other way round? At the time of writing, it seems less and less likely that any major developed economy will be able to inflate away its liabilities as happened in many cases in the 1920s and 1950s.[9] But why not? Milton Friedman's famous dictum that inflation is 'always and everywhere a monetary phenomenon' leaves unanswered the questions of who creates the excess money and why they do it. In practice, inflation is primarily a *political* phenomenon. Its likelihood is a function of factors like the content of elite education; competition (or the lack of it) in an economy; the character of the legal system; levels of violence; and the political decision-making process itself. Only by historical methods can we explain why, over the past thirty years, so many countries created forms of debt that, by design, cannot be inflated away; and why, as a result, the next generation will be saddled for life with liabilities incurred by their parents and grandparents.

In the same way, it is easy to explain why the financial crisis was caused by excessively large and leveraged financial institutions, but much harder to explain why, after more than four years of debate, the problem of 'too big to fail' banks has not been solved. Indeed, despite the passage of legislation covering literally thousands of pages, it has got markedly worse.[10] Today, a mere ten highly diversified financial institutions are responsible for three-quarters of total financial assets under management in the United States. Yet the country's largest banks are at least $50 billion short of meeting new capital requirements under the new 'Basel III' accords governing bank capital adequacy. Again, only a political and historical approach can explain why Western politicians today call simultaneously for banks to lend more money and for them to shrink their balance sheets.

Why is it now a hundred times more expensive to bring a new medicine to market than it was sixty years ago – a phenomenon Juan Enriquez has called 'Moore's Law* in reverse'? Why would the Food and Drug Administration probably prohibit the sale of table salt if it were put forward as a new pharmacological product (it is after all toxic in large doses)?[11] Why, to give another suggestive example, did it take an American journalist sixty-five days to get official permission (including, after a wait of up to five weeks, a Food Protection Certificate) to open a lemonade stand in New York City?[12] This is the kind of debilitating red tape that development economists often blame for poverty in Africa or Latin America. The rationale for the FDA's rigid standards is to avoid the sale of a drug like thalidomide. But the unintended consequence is almost certainly to allow many more people to die prematurely than would have died from side-effects under a less restrictive regime. We count and

---

* Moore's Law, formulated by Intel co-founder George Moore in 1965, predicted a doubling of the number of transistors that can be packed on to a computer chip every two years.

recount the costs of such side-effects. We do not count the costs of not allowing new drugs to be made available.

Why exactly has social mobility declined in the United States in the past thirty years, so that the probability has more than halved that a man born into the bottom 25 per cent of the income distribution will end his life in the top quartile?[13] Once the United States was famed as a land of opportunity, where a family could leap from 'rags to riches' in a generation. But today, if you are born to parents in the bottom income quintile, you have just a 5 per cent chance of getting into the top quintile without a college degree. What Charles Murray has called the 'cognitive elite', educated at exclusive private universities, intermarried and congregated in a few 'super zip codes', looks increasingly like a new caste, equipped with the wealth and power to override the effects of mean reversion in human reproduction, so that even their dimmer progeny inherit their lifestyle.[14]

The Stationary State

In two seldom quoted passages of *The Wealth of Nations*, Adam Smith described what he called 'the stationary state': the condition of a formerly wealthy country that had ceased to grow. What were the characteristics of this state? Significantly, Smith singled out its socially regressive character. First, wages for the majority of people were miserably low:

> Though the wealth of a country should be very great, yet if it has been long stationary, we must not expect to find the wages of labour very high in it . . . It is in the progressive state, while the society is advancing to the further acquisition, rather than when it has acquired its full complement of riches, that the condition of the labouring poor, of the great body of the people, seems to be the happiest and the most comfortable. It is hard in the stationary, and miserable in the declining state. The progressive state is in reality the cheerful and the hearty state to all the different orders of the society. The stationary is dull; the declining melancholy.[15]

The second hallmark of the stationary state was the ability of a corrupt and monopolistic elite to exploit the system of law and administration to their own advantage:

> In a country too, where, though the rich or the owners of large capitals enjoy a good deal of security, the poor or the owners of small capitals enjoy scarce any, but are liable, under the pretence of justice, to be pillaged and plundered at any time by the inferior mandarins, the quantity of stock employed in all the different branches of business transacted within it can never be equal to what the nature and extent of that business might admit. In every different branch, the oppression of the poor must establish the

monopoly of the rich, who, by engrossing the whole trade to themselves, will be able to make very large profits.[16]

I defy the Western reader not to feel an uneasy sense of recognition in contemplating those two passages.

In Smith's day, of course, it was China that had been 'long stationary': a once 'opulent' country that had simply ceased to grow. Smith blamed China's defective 'laws and institutions' – including its bureaucracy – for the stasis. More free trade, more encouragement for small business, less bureaucracy and less crony capitalism: these were Smith's prescriptions to cure Chinese stasis. He was a witness to what such reforms were doing in the late eighteenth century to galvanize the economy of the British Isles and its American colonies. Today, by contrast, if Smith could revisit those same places, he would behold an extraordinary reversal of fortunes. It is we Westerners who are in the stationary state, while China is growing faster than any other major economy in the world. The boot of economic history is on the other foot.

This book is about the causes of our stationary state. It is inspired by Smith's insight that both stagnation and growth are in large measure the results of 'laws and institutions'. Its central thesis is that what was true of China in Smith's day is true of large parts of the Western world in our time. It is our laws and institutions that are the problem. The Great Recession is merely a symptom of a more profound Great Degeneration.

The Four Black Boxes

To demonstrate that Western institutions have indeed degenerated, I am going to have to open up some long-sealed black boxes. The first is the one labelled 'democracy'. The second is labelled 'capitalism'. The third is 'the rule of law'. And the fourth is 'civil society'. Together, they are the key components of our civilization. I want to show that inside these political, economic, legal and social black boxes are highly complex sets of interlocking institutions. Like the circuit boards inside your computer or your smartphone, it is these institutions that make the gadget work. And if it stops working, it is probably because of a defect in the institutional wiring. You cannot understand what is wrong just by looking at the shiny casing. You need to look inside.

Perhaps, on reflection, that electronic metaphor is the wrong one. After all, most institutions evolve organically; they are not designed in California by the historical equivalent of Steve Jobs. A better analogy might be with the collective structures we see in the natural world. Beehives are the classic example. Ever since the satirist Bernard Mandeville's book *The Fable of The Bees: or, Private Vices, Public Benefits*, published in 1714, people have drawn parallels between humans in a market economy and bees in a hive. The parallel has its merits, as we shall see, though it is actually in our political organization rather than our economic organization that we most closely resemble bees (a point Mandeville well understood). The simple point is that institutions are to humans what hives are to bees. They are the structures within which we organize ourselves as groups. You know when you are inside one, just as a bee knows when it is in the hive. Institutions have boundaries, often walls. And, crucially, they have rules.

For some readers, I dare say, the word 'institution' still conjures up a Victorian vision of lunatic asylums: poor old Niall, he's in an *institution* now. That is not the kind of institution I mean. I am talking about, for example, political institutions, like the British Parliament or the American Congress. When we talk about 'democracy', we are in fact referring to a number of different interlocking institutions. People sticking pieces of paper into ballot boxes, yes. Their elected representatives making speeches and voting in a large assembly hall, yes. But those things alone do not automatically give you democracy. Outwardly, the legislators of countries like Russia and Venezuela are elected, but neither qualifies as a true democracy in the eyes of impartial observers, not to mention those of local opposition leaders.

Just as important as the act of putting crossed or stamped papers in ballot boxes are the institutions – usually parties – that nominate candidates for election. Just as important as the parties are the officials – civil servants, judges or ombudsmen – whose responsibility it is to ensure that the elections are fair. And then it matters hugely how the legislature itself actually operates. A body of elected representatives can be anything from a wholly sovereign entity, as the British Parliament was until European law began to encroach on it, to an impotent rubber stamp, like the old Supreme Soviet. Its members can stoutly uphold the interests of their constituents (including those who voted against them), or they can be in hock to the vested interests that financed their election campaigns.

In August 2011, as Colonel Gaddafi's regime in Libya was falling apart, a BBC correspondent in Benghazi spotted some remarkable graffiti on a wall. On the left side of the wall there was a classically straightforward revolutionary message: 'The tyrant should fall, he's a monster.' Direct and to the point. But on the right side, the message was anything but simple. It read: 'We want constitutional rule and for the president to have less authority and the four-year presidential term should not be extended.'[17] As that (quite correctly) suggests, the devil in any political transition lies in the detail of the constitution, not to mention the rules governing the constituent assembly that designs it.

How does the legislature stand relative to the executive and the judiciary? Most constitutions spell that out. But how do the organs of civilian government relate to the military, a question of burning importance in Egypt? Nor can one stop there. Modern nation-states have developed a whole range of institutions that were undreamed of as recently as a hundred years ago, dedicated to regulating economic and social life and redistributing income. The welfare state is not part of democracy as the ancient Athenians conceived of it. In bee terms, the welfare state seems to create an ever increasing number of dependent drones whom the worker-bees have to support. It also employs a great many bees simply to transfer resources from the workers to the drones. And it seeks to finance itself by accumulating claims on future bees, in the form of public debt. In Chapter 1, I will consider this and other distributional aspects of democracy. In particular, I will ask if we are witnessing a fundamental breakdown in what Edmund Burke called the partnership between the generations.

These days, nearly everyone claims to be democratic. I have even heard it claimed that the Chinese Communist Party is democratic. 'Capitalist', by contrast, is a word too often used as a term of abuse to be much heard in polite company. How do the institutions of the democratic state and those of the market economy relate to one another? Do corporations play an active part in politics, through lobbyists and campaign contributions? Do governments play an active part in economic life, through subsidies, tariffs and other market-distorting devices, or through regulation? What is the right balance to be struck between economic freedom and government regulation? Chapter 2 will address these issues. The specific question I ask is how far very complex regulation has become the disease of which it purports to be the cure, distorting and corrupting both the political and the economic process.

A crucial institutional check on both political and economic actors is the rule of law. It is inconceivable that either democracy or capitalism could function without an effective system of justice, where the rules devised by the legislature can be enforced, where the rights of the individual citizen can be upheld and where disputes between citizens or corporate entities can be resolved in a peaceful and rational manner. But which system of law is better: common law? or some other form? The rule of *sharia* is clearly very different from the rule of law as the English political philosopher John Locke understood it.

In some ways, the key to comparing different codes of law is what might be called 'the law of rules': the way that law itself is made. In some systems, like Islam, the rules have been prescribed in considerable detail, for eternity, by a divinely inspired prophet. According to the stricter schools of Muslim thought, they cannot be changed. In others, like the English common law, the rules evolve organically, as judges weigh up the competing claims of precedent and the changing needs of society. Chapter 3 will ask the question whether one system of law – in particular, the common law – is superior to the others. I will also ask how far the English-speaking world still enjoys an advantage in this respect. In particular, I want to warn that the rule of law is in danger – at least in parts of the 'Anglosphere' – of degenerating into something more like the rule of *lawyers*. Are Americans really better served by their legal system than Englishmen were by theirs at the time of Dickens's *Bleak House*?

Finally, there is civil society. Properly understood, it is the realm of voluntary associations: institutions established by citizens with an objective other than private profit.

These can range from schools – although in modern times most educational institutions have been absorbed into the public sector – to clubs dedicated to the full range of human activities, from aeronautics to zoology. Once again we encounter the importance of rules, though here they may seem trivial, like the obligation on members of most London clubs to wear ties and keep their jackets on at dinner, even on a sweltering-hot evening.

There was a time when the average Briton or American belonged to a startlingly large number of clubs and other voluntary societies. It was one of the features of the English-speaking world that most impressed the great French political theorist Alexis de Tocqueville. But in Chapter 4 I shall ask why that is no longer true, and how far it is possible for a truly free society to flourish in the absence of the kind of vibrant civil society we used to take for granted. Are the new social networks of the internet in any sense a substitute for traditional associational life? I shall argue that they are not.

Why Institutions Fail

If we are like bees in the realm of politics, playing our assigned parts in an essentially hierarchical hive, we have more freedom of action in the economic sphere. There, our institutions recall the wildlife of the Serengeti, the 'endless plains' of northern Tanzania and southern Kenya. Some of us are wildebeest, grazing as we move in the herd. Others of us (rather fewer) are predators. I am afraid there are some scavengers and parasites, too. The whole thing is an ecosystem in which Darwinian forces are constantly at work, naturally selecting the fittest from the unfit. Likewise, in civil society, we form our groups and bands rather in the way that chimpanzees and baboons do. Like the clubs we humans used to be so fond of joining, a baboon troop has its rules and its hierarchies.

Of course, there is no law governing the wild animals of Africa other than the proverbial law of the jungle. We humans are different. While part of our lives may be spent in a Darwinian struggle, we do expect there to be rules: rules to constrain our rulers; rules to constrain the predators and parasites who prey on the herbivores. The rule of law, properly understood, has no real analogue in the non-human world. The nearest I can think of is the man-made infrastructure that surrounds us, shaping the landscape, sheltering us and constraining us. The law sets parameters in the same way that walls and fences do. This way is much too steep; that way you risk drowning. Some systems of law resemble centrally planned cities: like Moscow, with its over-wide avenues and homogenizing apartment blocks. Others are more like London: an unplanned complex of irregular streets and idiosyncratic buildings, the organic product of centuries of building and rebuilding by private and public property owners.

What makes humans so very interesting to study – the reason I am an historian and not a zoologist – is that our lives combine all of these elements. We exist, simultaneously, in a bewildering number of institutions. We are at one and the same time citizens, residents and taxpayers of states; shareholders, managers or employees; litigants, defendants, judges and jurors; club members, officials and trustees. *Homo economicus* is only one of the many parts we play.

The key point is that not all sets of institutions, when you add up the sum of the parts, are equal. There are good and bad combinations. In some sets of institutions, people can flourish freely as individuals, as families, as communities. That is because the institutions effectively incentivize us to do good things – like, for example, inventing new and more efficient ways of working, or co-operating with our neighbours rather than trying to murder them. Conversely, there are institutional frameworks that have the opposite effect: incentivizing bad behaviour like killing people who annoy us, or stealing property we covet, or idling away our time. Where bad institutions pertain, people get stuck in vicious circles of ignorance, ill health, poverty and, often, violence. Unfortunately, history suggests that there are more of these suboptimal frameworks than there are optimal frameworks. A really good set of institutions is hard to achieve. Bad institutions, by contrast, are easy to get stuck in. And this is why most countries have been poor for most of history, as well as illiterate, unhealthy and bloody.

I admire contemporary social scientific work that distinguishes between 'open' and 'closed' sets of institutions,[18] but as an historian I find that distinction too simplistic. For one of the puzzles of modern history is that successful societies – like eighteenth-century England – often had institutions that today most people would be inclined to condemn. Already by the time of the Victorians, Hanoverian England looked shockingly corrupt in retrospect. And even in the 1850s, to Dickens, England's rule of law was still an object of derision, not admiration. Moreover, the historical approach reveals a point that is often overlooked. It is certainly desirable that societies with bad institutions should get better ones. We see that process going on today all over the world, in much of Asia, in parts of South America and even in Africa. But there is a more insidious process that is going on at the same time, whereby societies with good institutions gradually get worse ones. Why is this? Who exactly are the enemies of the rule of law, the people responsible for the marked deterioration that I detect in our institutions on both sides of the Atlantic?

My answers to these questions owe a considerable debt to a now large body of academic literature. Major influences on my thinking include Douglass North, who won the Nobel Prize for Economics for his work on institutions;

the pre-eminent economist of modern Africa, Paul Collier, author of *The Bottom Billion* and *Plundered Planet*; Hernando de Soto, the Peruvian economist and author of *The Mystery of Capital*; Andrei Shleifer and his numerous co-authors, who have pioneered an economic approach to the comparative study of legal systems; and Jim Robinson and Daron Acemoglu, whose book *Why Nations Fail* asks similar questions to the ones that interest me. I owe these and the other scholars acknowledged in the notes a deep intellectual debt.

However, they would be the first to agree that much more attention has been paid to the question of why poor nations stay poor, as opposed to the question of why rich nations revert to poverty, a somewhat less common phenomenon. My concern here is not with economic development but rather with the opposite process of institutional degeneration. My over-arching question is: what exactly has gone wrong in the Western world in our time? I answer that question in the belief that, until we understand the true nature of our degeneration, we will be wasting our time, applying quack remedies to mere symptoms. I am also actuated by the fear that, paradoxically, the economic stationary state may have dangerously dynamic political consequences.

1. The Human Hive

Explaining the Great Divergence

'Nature ... is a thynge of great myghte and efficacye,' wrote the English humanist Richard Taverner in his *Garden of Wysdome*, 'but surely institution or bringynge up, is moche mightier, whiche is hable to amende, reforme & strengthen a croked and evyll nature, and turn the same into a good nature.'[1] Taverner's words sum up what is fast becoming a compelling consensus: that institutions – in the broadest sense of the term – determine modern historical outcomes, more than natural forces like the weather, geography or even the incidence of disease.

Why, after around 1500, did Western civilization – as found in the quarrelsome petty states of Western Eurasia and their colonies of settlement in the New World – fare so much better than other civilizations? From the 1500s until the late 1970s, there was an astonishing divergence in

Ratios of US to Chinese and UK to Indian per capita GDP since 1500

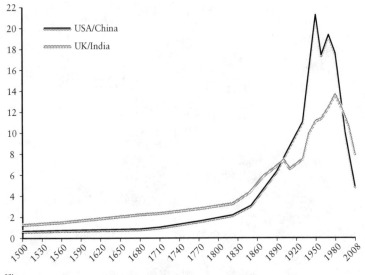

Figure 1.1

Source: Angus Maddison, 'Statistics on World Population, GDP and Per Capita GDP, 1–2008 AD': http://www.ggdc.net/MADDISON/Historical_Statistics/vertical-file_02-2010.xls.

global living standards, as Westerners became far richer than, well, Resterners. As recently as 300 years ago, the average Chinese was probably still a bit better off than the average North American. By 1978, the average American was at least twenty-two times richer than the average Chinese (see Figure 1.1).[2] History's great divergence was not just economic. It was also a divergence in terms of longevity and health. As recently as 1960, life expectancy in China was in the low forties, whereas already in the United States it had reached seventy.[3] Westerners dominated the realm of science, as well as that of popular culture. To an astonishing degree they also continued to rule the world even after the demise of the dozen or so formal empires which, at their zenith, had covered nearly three-fifths of the world's land surface and population and accounted for at least three-quarters of global economic output. It was a conceit of the Cold War to refer to the Soviet empire as 'the East'; in reality it was the last European empire to rule over large tracts of Asia.

How are we to explain this, the ultimate global imbalance, which placed a minority of mankind – at most a fifth – in such a position of material and political dominance over the rest? It seems implausible that it was due to some innate superiority of Europeans, as the racial theorists of the nineteenth and twentieth centuries often argued. The gene pool was surely not so different in the year 500, when the western end of Eurasia was entering a period of nearly a thousand years of relative stagnation. Likewise, the climate, topography and natural resources of Europe were much the same in 1500 as they had been in 500. Throughout the Dark Ages and medieval period, European civilization showed no obvious sign of outperforming the great Oriental empires. With all due respect to Jared Diamond, geography and its agricultural consequences may explain why Eurasia did better than other parts of the world; but they can't explain why the western end of Eurasia did so much better than the eastern end after 1500.[4]

Nor can we explain the great divergence in terms of

imperialism; the other civilizations did plenty of that before Europeans began crossing oceans and conquering. For the historian Kenneth Pomeranz, who coined the phrase 'the great divergence', it was really just a matter of luck. Europeans were fortunate enough to stumble on the so-called 'ghost acres' of the Caribbean, which were soon providing the peoples of the Atlantic metropoles with abundant sugar, a compact source of calories unavailable to most Asians. Europeans were also fortunate to have more readily accessible deposits of coal.[5] Yet this argument leaves unanswered the questions of why the Chinese were not as assiduous as Europeans in the search for colonial ghost acres overseas; and why they were unable to solve the technical challenges of mining coal the way the British did.

I believe the best answers to the question of what caused the great divergence focus on the role of institutions. For example, Douglass North, John Wallis and Barry Weingast distinguish between two phases or patterns of human organization.[6] The first is what they call the natural state or 'limited access pattern', characterized by:

- a slow-growing economy;
- relatively few non-state organizations;
- a small and quite centralized government, operating without the consent of the governed; and
- social relationships organized along personal and dynastic lines.

The second is the 'open access pattern', characterized by:

— a faster-growing economy;
— a rich and vibrant civil society with lots of organizations;
— a bigger, more decentralized government; and
— social relationships governed by impersonal forces like the rule of law, involving secure property rights, fairness and (at least in theory) equality.

In their account, West European states – led by England – were the first to make the transition from 'limited access' to 'open access'. In order to do this, a country has to 'develop institutional arrangements that enable elites to create the possibility of impersonal intra-elite relationships' and then to 'create and sustain new incentives for elites to success-fully open access within the elite'. At this point, 'Elites transform their personal privileges into impersonal rights. All elites are given the right to form organizations . . . at that point, the logic . . . has changed from the natural state logic of rent-creation through privileges to the open access logic of rent-erosion through entry.'

Between the Conquest and the Glorious Revolution, England went from being a 'fragile' natural state to being a 'basic' one and then a 'mature one', characterized by an 'extensive set of institutions governing, regulating, and enforcing property rights in land capable of supporting impersonal exchange among elites'. The rule of law for elites was one of the three 'doorstep conditions', prior to the transition to an open-access system, the others being the emergence of 'perpetually lived organizations in the public [and] private sphere[s]' and the 'consolidated control of the military'. For North, Wallis and Weingast, the decisive breakthrough to open access came with the American and French Revolutions, which saw the spread of incorporation in various forms, and the legitimation of open competition in both the economic and political spheres. At each stage of the argument, then, their emphasis is on institutions, beginning with changes in English land law after the eleventh century, and culminating with changes in the legal treatment of corporate entities in the nineteenth century.

In a similar vein, Francis Fukuyama's *Origins of Political Order* defines 'the three components of a modern political order' as 'a strong and capable state, the state's subordination to a rule of law and government accountability to all citizens'.[7] These three components came together for the first time in Western Europe, with England once again the trailblazer (though Fukuyama gives credit to the Netherlands, Denmark and Sweden for not being far behind). Why Europe and not Asia? Because, says Fukuyama, the idiosyncratic development of Western Christendom tended to undercut the importance of extended families or clans.

In their book *Why Nations Fail*, Daron Acemoglu and Jim Robinson make a striking comparison between Egypt today and England in the late seventeenth century:

The reason that Britain is richer than Egypt is because in 1688 ... England ... had a revolution that transformed the politics and thus the economics of the nation. People fought for and won more political rights and used them to expand their economic opportunities. The result was a fundamentally different political and economic trajectory, culminating in the Industrial Revolution.[8]

In their terms, England was the first country to move to having 'inclusive' or 'pluralistic' rather than 'extractive' political institutions. Note that other West European societies – for instance, Spain – failed to do this. As a result, the outcomes of European colonization in North and South America were radically different. The English exported inclusive institutions; the Spaniards were content to superimpose their extractive ones on top of those they took over from the Aztecs and Incas.

The imperial context also reveals the difference between the institutional argument and the older cultural interpretation – first formulated by Max Weber, later revived by David Landes – that there was some link between Protestantism and the 'spirit of capitalism'. Unlike the Nazi in Hanns Johst's play *Schlageter*, I do not reach for my revolver when I hear the word culture, but I do issue a polite health warning. It is very tempting to attribute historical agency to an amalgam of ideas and norms – Greek philosophy, the Hebrew Commandments, Roman law, Christ's ethics, the doctrine of Luther and Calvin – called something like 'Judaeo-Christian culture'. But there is a real risk of cherry-picking here. Somehow no really terrible Western ideas like, say, witch-burning or communism ever get mentioned, though they seem just as plausibly the products of Judaeo-Christian culture as the spirit of capitalism. In any case, while culture may instil norms, institutions create incentives. Britons versed in much the same culture behaved very differently depending on whether they emigrated to New England or worked for the East India Company in Bengal. In the former case we find inclusive institutions, in the latter extractive ones.

Glorious Institutions

The debate about the causes of the great divergence is of more than merely historical interest. Understanding Western success helps us to frame some rather more urgent questions about the recent past, the present and possible futures. One reason the institutional argument is so compelling is that it also seems to offer a good explanation for the failure of most non-Western countries, until the later twentieth century, to achieve sustained economic growth. Acemoglu and Robinson illustrate the power of institutions relative to geography and culture by describing the city of Nogales, which is bisected by the US–Mexican border. The difference in living standards between the two halves is shocking.[9] The same point can be made with regard to the two great experiments run during the Cold War. Essentially, we took two peoples – the Koreans and the Germans – and divided them in two. South Koreans and West Germans got capitalist institutions; North Koreans and East Germans got communist ones. The divergence that occurred in the space of just a few decades was enormous. Their analysis makes Acemoglu and Robinson sceptical that China has yet made the decisive breakthrough to sustainable growth. In their view, Chinese market reforms remain subject to the decisions of an exclusive and extractive elite, which continues to determine the allocation of key resources.

Development economists – notably Paul Collier – have been thinking in these terms for some time.[10] The case of Botswana seems to illustrate the point that even a sub-Saharan African economy can achieve sustained growth if its people are not plagued by chronic corruption and/or civil war like, say, the Democratic Republic of Congo. Unlike most post-colonial African states, Botswana succeeded in establishing inclusive not extractive institutions when it gained its independence. The Peruvian economist Hernando de Soto is another who has been arguing for years that institutions are what matter.[11] By slogging away in the shanty towns of Lima, Port-au-Prince, Cairo and Manila, he and his researchers established that, though their incomes are low, the poor of the world have a surprisingly large amount of property. The problem is that this property is not legally recognized as theirs. It is nearly all held 'extra-legally'. This is not because the poor are tax-dodgers. As de Soto makes clear, the black economy has its own kind of taxation – protection rackets and the like – which make legality positively attractive. It is just that getting legal title to a house or a workshop is well-nigh impossible.

As an experiment, de Soto and his team tried to establish a small garment workshop on the outskirts of Lima on a legal basis. It took them a staggering 289 days to do so. And when they tried to secure legal authorization to build a house on state-owned land, it took even longer: six years and eleven months, during which they had to deal with fifty-two different government offices. Dysfunctional institutions like these, de Soto argues, are what force the poor to live outside the law. We should not imagine that the extra-legal economy is marginal. One of the most memorable findings of de Soto's book *The Mystery of Capital* is that the total value of the real estate held (but not legally owned) by the poor of developing countries amounts to $9.3 trillion. Yet, in the absence of legal titles and a working system of property law, this is all so much 'dead capital': 'like water in a lake high up in the Andes – an untapped stock of potential energy'. It cannot be efficiently used to generate wealth. Only with a working system of property rights can a house become collateral, can its value be properly established by the market, can it easily be bought and sold.

Since de Soto published *The Mystery of Capital*, revolutions in countries like Tunisia and Egypt have provided compelling evidence in support of his approach. He sees the 'Arab Spring' primarily as a revolt by frustrated would-be entrepreneurs against corrupt, rent-seeking regimes that preyed on their efforts to accumulate capital. The prime example is the story of the twenty-six-year-old Tarek Mohamed Bouazizi, who burned himself to death in front of the governor's offices in the town of Sidi Bouzid in December 2010.[12] Bouazizi killed himself precisely one hour after a policewoman, backed by two municipal officers, had seized from him two crates of pears, a crate of bananas, three crates of apples and a second-hand electronic weight scale worth $179. Those scales were his only capital. He did not have legal title to his family's home, which might otherwise have served as collateral for his business. His economic existence depended on the 'fees' he paid to officials to allow him to operate his fruit-stand on two square yards of public land. Their arbitrary act of expropriation cost Mohamed Bouazizi his livelihood and his life. But his self-immolation sparked a revolution – though how glorious a revolution remains to be seen. It will depend on how far new constitutional arrangements in countries like Tunisia and Egypt achieve the shift from an extractive to an inclusive state, from the arbitrary power of rent-seeking elites to the rule of law for all.

If de Soto's approach is right, then it does make a great deal of sense to explain the success of the West after the 1500s in terms of institutions, and particularly the rule of law. For what was at the heart of England's seventeenth-century battles over Parliamentary power was surely the protection of individuals from arbitrary expropriation by the Crown. To specialist historians, of course, all this smacks suspiciously of the old Whig interpretation of history that Herbert Butterfield once held up to ridicule. Yet none of the authors I have been quoting takes a naively determinist view of the historical process. Far from being a story of teleological inevitability, these are authentically evolutionary narratives, in which contingency plays a major role. England was not preordained by Providence to become (as in *1066 and All That*) 'top nation'. Only a series of near-run things averted an absolutist outcome in the seventeenth century. There were, after all, rebellions in 1692, 1694, 1696, 1704, 1708 and 1722, and a civil war in 1715 – not forgetting the Jacobite Rising of 1745.[13]

The real question is how decisive an institutional break occurred in 1688. The majority of historians would say: not very. The Glorious Revolution, they argue, was backward looking, 'conservationist', with minimal consequences outside the narrow sphere of aristocratic power and patronage.[14] I think this is too parochial a view. The 1689 Bill of Rights – the Act Declaring the Rights and Liberties of the Subject – states (among other things):

– that levying money for or to the use of the Crown
  by pretence of prerogative, without grant of
  Parliament, for longer time, or in other manner
  than the same is or shall be granted, is illegal;

- that election of members of Parliament ought to be free;
- that the freedom of speech and debates or proceedings in Parliament ought not to be impeached or questioned in any court or place out of Parliament; and
- that for redress of all grievances, and for the amending, strengthening and preserving of the laws, Parliaments ought to be held frequently.

With all due respect to the specialists, I think this does deserve to be seen as an historical turning point, even if religious prejudice (anti-Catholicism) loomed as large as constitutional principle at the time.

True, the 'rights and liberties of the subject' set out in the 1689 Bill of Rights were conceived at the time as ancient rather than novel. But the consequences of the Glorious Revolution really were new, not least in the way Parliaments after 1689 set about energetically legislating for economic development, protecting the infant textile industry, encouraging the enclosure of common land, promoting turnpike roads and canals. Even war became an increasingly profitable activity as the Whigs launched their bid for global commercial supremacy.[15] The sequence is clear: first the Glorious Revolution, then agricultural improvement, then imperial expansion, then industrial revolution.

The institutional argument is even more compelling when we take a comparative approach. None of the institutional changes I am talking about happened in Ming or Qing China, where the power of the Emperor and his officials remained unrestrained by semi-autonomous corporate bodies or representative assemblies. Asia had merchants; it did not have companies, much less parliaments.[16] Institutions as they evolved in the Ottoman Empire were also significantly different in ways that hampered capital formation and economic development, as Timur Kuran has argued. This was because Islamic law took a fundamentally different approach to partnership, inheritance, questions of debt and corporate personalities from the legal systems that developed in Western Europe. Islam had *waqfs*, unincorporated trusts established by individuals, but not banks.[17]

The Inglorious Revolution

So if institutional evolution is the key to understanding Western ascendancy as well as enduring poverty in Africa and elsewhere, is this also how we should understand what is surely the most astonishing trend of our lifetimes: the end of the great divergence, and the advent of a great reconvergence between West and East? I think it is. What we need to do is to apply the insights of the institutional school of economic history to our own time – indeed, to our own Western societies.

Writing in the 1770s, it seemed obvious to Adam Smith

that the reasons for China's puzzling 'stationary state' of economic stagnation lay in its 'laws and institutions'. Could it be, by the same token, that the economic, social and political difficulties of the Western world today reflect a degeneration of our once world-beating institutions? There certainly seems little doubt that the West is experiencing a relative decline unlike anything we have seen in half a millennium. Having been more than twenty times richer than the average Chinese in 1978, the average American is now just five times richer. In a whole range of dimensions, the gap between the West and the Rest has narrowed dramatically. In terms of life expectancy and educational attainment, for example, some Asian countries are now ahead of most in the West. According to the 2009 OECD PISA study, the gap in mathematical attainment between the teenagers of the Shanghai district of China and those of the United States is now as big as the gap between American teenagers and Tunisians.[18]

In some ways, it is easy to explain non-Western success. China has belatedly followed a number of other East Asian countries – the first was Japan – in downloading most (not all) of what I have called the 'killer applications' of Western civilization: economic competition, the scientific revolution, modern medicine, the consumer society and the work ethic.[19] Copying the Western model of industrialization and urbanization tends to work if your entrepreneurs have the right incentives, your labour force is basically healthy, literate and numerate, and your bureaucracy is reasonably efficient. So in what follows I am going to say relatively little about what has gone right in the rest of the world. What interests me here is what has gone wrong in the West.

Most commentators who address this question tend to concern themselves with phenomena like excessive debt, mismanaged banks and widening inequality. To my mind, however, these are nothing more than symptoms of an underlying institutional malaise: an Inglorious Revolution, if you like, which is undoing the achievements of half a millennium of Western institutional evolution.

Debt and the English

The title of this chapter –'The Human Hive' – is an allusion to Mandeville's poem, *The Fable of the Bees*. Mandeville's central point was that societies with the right institutions can flourish even when the individuals who live in them misbehave. It was not biblical virtue that made eighteenth-century England richer than almost anywhere in the world, but rather secular vices. It was just that these vices had what economists like to call 'positive network externalities' precisely because the institutions of British society at that time were favourable to saving, investment and innovation.

After the Glorious Revolution of 1688, as we have seen, the monarch was subordinated to Parliament. Not only did the Whigs who dominated the new regime usher in an age of agricultural improvement, commercial growth and imperial expansion. Financial institutions also developed rapidly: William of Orange brought more than just Protestantism with him from Holland; he also brought templates for a central bank and a stock market. Meanwhile, numerous associations, societies and clubs encouraged scientific and technological innovation. As Robert Allen has shown, the specifically British combination of cheap coal and dear labour encouraged innovation in productivity-enhancing technologies, especially in textile production.[20] But the institutions provided the indispensable framework for all this. Here is Mandeville's version:

> A Spacious Hive well stock'd with Bees,
> That lived in Luxury and Ease;
> And yet as fam'd for Laws and Arms,
> As yielding large and early Swarms;
> Was counted the great Nursery
> Of Sciences and Industry.
> No Bees had better Government,
> More Fickleness, or less Content.
> They were not Slaves to Tyranny,
> Nor ruled by wild Democracy;
> But Kings, that could not wrong, because
> Their Power was circumscrib'd by Laws.

There was one particular institution that decisively altered the trajectory of English history. In a seminal article published in 1989, North and Weingast argued that the real significance of the Glorious Revolution lay in the credibility that it gave the English state as a sovereign borrower. From 1689, Parliament controlled and improved taxation, audited royal expenditures, protected private property rights and effectively prohibited debt default. This arrangement, they argued, was 'self-enforcing', not least because property owners were overwhelmingly the class represented in Parliament. As a result, the English state was able to borrow money on a scale that had previously been impossible because of the sovereign's habit of defaulting or arbitrarily taxing or expropriating.[21] The late seventeenth and early eighteenth century thus inaugurated a period of rapid accumulation of public debt without any rise in borrowing costs – rather the reverse.

This was in fact a benign development. Not only did it enable England to become Great Britain and, indeed, the British Empire, by giving the English state unrivalled financial resources for making – and winning – war. By accustoming the wealthy to investment in paper securities, it also paved the way for a financial revolution that would channel English savings into everything from canals to railways, commerce to colonization, ironworks to textile mills. Though the national debt grew enormously in the course of England's many wars with France, reaching a peak of more than 260 per cent of GDP in the decade after 1815, this leverage earned a handsome return, because on the other side of the balance sheet, acquired largely with a debt-financed navy, was a global empire. Moreover, in the century after Waterloo, the debt was successfully reduced with a combination of sustained growth and primary budget surpluses. There was no default. There was no inflation. And Britannia bestrode the globe.

The Partnership between the Generations

In the rest of this chapter, I want to make an argument about our modern representative government – and what ails it. My starting assumption is the conventional one that it is generally better for government to be in some way representative of the governed than not. This is not just because democracy is a good thing *per se*, as Amartya Sen has argued, but also because a representative government is more likely than an authoritarian government to be responsive to shifting popular preferences and is therefore less likely to make the kind of horrendous mistakes authoritarian rulers often make. Those today who dismiss Western democracy as 'broken' – and I hear their lamentations with growing frequency – are wrong to yearn for some kind of Beijing model of a one-party state in which decisions are taken by technocrats on the basis of five-year plans. It was the same system that gave China both Special Economic Zones and the One-Child Policy: the former a success, the latter a disaster, the full costs of which are as yet incalculable.

But the critics of Western democracy are right to discern that something is amiss with our political institutions. The most obvious symptoms of the malaise are the huge debts we have managed to accumulate in recent decades, which (unlike in the past) cannot largely be blamed on wars. According to the International Monetary Fund, the gross government debt of Greece will reach 182 per cent of GDP in 2013. For Italy the figure is 128, for Ireland 119, for Portugal 124 and for the United States 112. Britain's debt is approaching 93 per cent. Japan – a special case as the first non-Western country to adopt Western institutions – is the world leader, with a mountain of government debt approaching 245 per cent of GDP, more than triple what it was twenty years ago.* Even more striking are the ratios of debt to government revenue, which after all is where the interest and redemption payments must come from (see Figure 1.2).

Often these debts get discussed as if they themselves are the problem, and the result is a rather sterile argument between proponents of 'austerity' and 'stimulus'. I want to suggest that they are a consequence of a more profound institutional malfunction.

---

* Note that I leave aside the very large private debts that have been incurred by households and by financial and non-financial corporations. If one adds these together with the government debts, the burdens have no precedent in history: Japan 512 per cent of GDP, Britain 507 per cent, France 346 per cent, Italy 314 per cent, the United States 279 per cent, Germany 278 per cent.

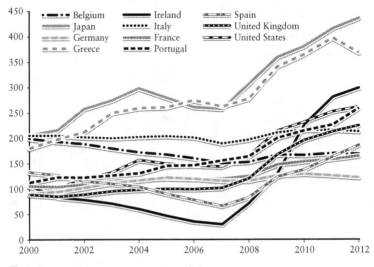

General government net debt as a percentage
of revenue, 2000–2012

Figure 1.2
Source: International Monetary Fund, World Economic Outlook Database,
April 2012: http://www.imf.org/external/pubs/ft/weo/2012/01/weodata/
index.aspx.

The heart of the matter is the way public debt allows the
current generation of voters to live at the expense of those
as yet too young to vote or as yet unborn. In this regard,
the statistics commonly cited as government debt are
themselves deeply misleading, for they encompass only
the sums owed by governments in the form of bonds. The
rapidly rising quantity of these bonds certainly implies a
growing charge on those in employment, now and in the
future, since – even if the current low rates of interest
enjoyed by the biggest sovereign borrowers persist – the

amount of money needed to service the debt must inexorably rise. But the official debts in the form of bonds do not include the often far larger unfunded liabilities of welfare schemes like – to give the biggest American programmes – Medicare, Medicaid and Social Security.

The best available estimate for the difference between the net present value of federal government liabilities and the net present value of future federal revenues is $200 trillion, nearly thirteen times the debt as stated by the US Treasury. Notice that these figures, too, are incomplete, since they omit the unfunded liabilities of state and local governments, which are estimated to be around $38 trillion.[22] These mind-boggling numbers represent nothing less than a vast claim by the generation currently retired or about to retire on their children and grandchildren, who are obliged by current law to find the money in the future, by submitting either to substantial increases in taxation or to drastic cuts in other forms of public expenditure.

To illustrate the magnitude of the American problem, the economist Laurence Kotlikoff calculates that to eliminate the federal government's fiscal gap would require an immediate 64 per cent increase in all federal taxes or an immediate 40 per cent cut in all federal expenditures.[23] When Kotlikoff compiled his 'generational accounts' for the United Kingdom more than a decade ago, he estimated (on what proved to be the correct assumption that the then government would increase welfare and healthcare spending) that there would need to be a 31 per cent increase in income tax revenues and a 46 per cent increase in national insurance revenues to close the fiscal gap.[24]

In his *Reflections on the Revolution in France* (1790), Edmund Burke wrote that the real social contract is not Jean-Jacques Rousseau's contract between the sovereign and the people or 'general will', but the 'partnership' between the generations. In his words:

> one of the first and most leading principles on which the commonwealth and the laws are consecrated is, lest the temporary possessors and life-renters in it, unmindful of what they have received from their ancestors or of what is due to their posterity, should act as if they were the entire masters, that they should not think it among their rights to cut off the entail or commit waste on the inheritance by destroying at their pleasure the whole original fabric of their society, hazarding to leave to those who come after them a ruin instead of an habitation – and teaching these successors as little to respect their contrivances as they had themselves respected the institutions of their forefathers . . . SOCIETY is indeed a contract . . . the state . . . is . . . a partnership not only between those who are living, but between those who are living, those who are dead, and those who are to be born.

In the enormous inter-generational transfers implied by current fiscal policies we see a shocking and perhaps unparalleled breach of precisely that partnership.

I want to suggest that the biggest challenge facing mature

democracies is how to restore the social contract between the generations. But I recognize that the obstacles to doing so are daunting. Not the least of these is that the young find it quite hard to compute their own long-term economic interests. It is surprisingly easy to win the support of young voters for policies that would ultimately make matters even worse for them, like maintaining defined benefit pensions for public employees. If young Americans knew what was good for them, they would all be fans of Paul Ryan.* A second problem is that today's Western democracies now play such a large part in redistributing income that politicians who argue for cutting expenditures nearly always run into the well-organized opposition of one or both of two groups: recipients of public sector pay and recipients of government benefits.

Is there a constitutional solution to this problem? The simplistic answer – which has already been adopted in a number of American states as well as in Germany – is some kind of balanced-budget amendment, which would reduce the discretion of lawmakers to engage in deficit spending, much as the practice of giving central banks independence reduced lawmakers' discretion over monetary policy. The trouble is that the experience of the financial

---

* A few months after the March 2012 coup in Mali, I was struck by the following observation by an American anthropologist in Bamako: 'There is an inchoate notion among young people that the political class is taking away their futures.' At some point this same inchoate notion will start playing a major role in US politics.

crisis has substantially strengthened the case for using the government deficit as a tool to stimulate the economy in times of recession, to say nothing of the wider case for deficit-financed public investment in infrastructure. In 2011, following a German lead, continental European leaders sought to solve that problem by resolving to limit only their structural deficits, leaving themselves room for man-oeuvre for cyclical deficits as and when required. But the problem with this 'fiscal compact' is that only two Euro-zone governments are currently below the mandated 0.5 per cent of GDP ceiling, most have structural deficits at least four times too large, and experience suggests that any government that tries seriously to reduce its structural deficit ends up being driven from power.

It is perhaps not surprising that a majority of current voters should support policies of inter-generational inequity, especially when older voters are so much more likely to vote than younger voters. But what if the net result of passing the buck for the baby-boomers' profligacy is not just unfair to the young but economically deleterious for everyone? What if uncertainty about the future is already starting to weigh on the present? As Carmen Reinhart and Ken Rogoff have suggested, it is hard to believe that developed-country growth rates will be unaffected by mountains of debt in excess of 90 per cent of GDP.[25] Anxiety about a fast-approaching 'fiscal cliff' may have been one reason why the US economy did not achieve 'escape velocity' in 2012.

Unsettling Accounts

It seems as if there are only two possible ways out of this mess. In the good but less likely scenario, the proponents of reform succeed, through a heroic effort of leadership, in persuading not only the young but also a significant proportion of their parents and grandparents to vote for a more responsible fiscal policy. As I have already explained, this is very hard to do. But I believe there is a way of making such leadership more likely to succeed, and that is to alter the way in which governments account for their finances.

The present system is, to put it bluntly, fraudulent. There are no regularly published and accurate official balance sheets. Huge liabilities are simply hidden from view. Not even the current income and expenditure statements can be relied upon. No legitimate business could possibly carry on in this fashion. The last corporation to publish financial statements this misleading was Enron.

There is in fact a better way. Public sector balance sheets can and should be drawn up so that the liabilities of governments can be compared with their assets. That would help clarify the difference between deficits to finance investment and deficits to finance current consumption. Governments should also follow the lead of business and adopt the Generally Accepted Accounting Principles. And, above all, generational accounts should be prepared on a regular basis to make absolutely clear the inter-generational implications of current policy.

If we do not do these things – if we do not embark on a wholesale reform of government finance – then I am afraid we are going to end up with the bad, but more likely, second scenario. Western democracies are going to carry on in their current feckless fashion until, one after another, they follow Greece and other Mediterranean economies into the fiscal death spiral that begins with a loss of credibility, continues with a rise in borrowing costs, and ends as governments are forced to impose spending cuts and higher taxes at the worst possible moment. In this scenario, the endgame involves some combination of default and inflation. We all end up as Argentina.

There is, it is true, a third possibility, and that is what we now see in Japan and the United States, maybe also in the United Kingdom. The debt continues to mount up. But deflationary fears, central bank bond purchases and a 'flight to safety' from the rest of the world keep government borrowing costs down at unprecedented lows. The trouble with this scenario is that it also implies low to zero growth over decades: a new version of Adam Smith's stationary state. Only now it is the West that is stationary.

As our economic difficulties have worsened, we voters have struggled to find the appropriate scapegoat. We blame the politicians whose hard lot it is to bring public finances under control. But we also like to blame bankers and financial markets, as if their reckless lending were to blame for our reckless borrowing. We bay for tougher regulation, though not of ourselves. This brings me to the subject of my second chapter. In it, I shall turn from the realm of politics to the realm of economics – from the human hive of democracy to the Darwinian jungle of the market – to ask if here, too, we are witnessing a tendency towards institutional degeneration in the Western world.

In this chapter, I have tried to show that excessive public debts are a symptom of the breakdown of the social contract between the generations. In my next I shall ask if excessively complex government regulation of markets is in fact the disease of which it purports to be the cure. The rule of law has many enemies, as we shall see. But among its most dangerous foes are the authors of very long and convoluted laws.

2. The Darwinian Economy

The Deregulation Illusion

What is the biggest problem facing the world economy today? To listen to some people, you might think the correct answer is insufficient financial regulation. According to a number of influential commentators, the origins of the financial crisis that began in 2007 – and still does not seem to be over – lie in decisions dating back to the early 1980s that led to a substantial deregulation of financial markets. In the good old days, we are told, banking was 'boring'. In the United States, the Glass–Steagall Act of 1933 separated the activities of commercial and investment banks until its supposedly fateful repeal in 1999.

'Reagan-era legislative changes essentially ended New Deal restrictions on mortgage lending,' the Princeton economist Paul Krugman has written. 'It was only after the Reagan deregulation that thrift gradually disappeared from the American way of life . . .' It was 'also mainly thanks to Reagan-era deregulation' that the financial system 'took on too much risk with too little capital'.[1] In another of his newspaper columns, Krugman looked back fondly to a 'long period of stability after World War II'. This was 'based on a combination of deposit insurance, which eliminated the threat of bank runs, and strict regulation of bank balance sheets, including both limits on risky lending and limits on leverage, the extent to which banks were allowed to finance investments with borrowed funds'.[2] It was indeed a golden age: the 'era of boring banking was also an era of spectacular economic progress'.[3] 'Overall business productivity in America grew faster in the post-war generation, an era in which banks were tightly regulated and private equity barely existed, than it has since our political system decided that greed was good.'[4]

Krugman is by no means a lone voice. Simon Johnson has written a devastating account of financial recklessness in his book *Thirteen Bankers*.[5] Even Chicago's Richard Posner has joined the chorus calling for a restoration of Glass–Steagall.[6] To cap it all, the architect of the behemoth Citigroup, Sandy Weill himself, has now recanted.[7] The first draft of the history of the financial crisis is in, and here is what it says: deregulation was to blame. Unfettered after 1980, financial markets ran amok, banks blew up and then had to be bailed out. Now they must be fettered once again.

As will become clear, it is not my purpose to whitewash the bankers. But I do believe this story is mostly wrong. For one thing, it is hard to think of a major event in the US crisis – beginning with the failures of Bear Stearns and Lehman Brothers – that could not equally well have happened with Glass–Steagall still in force. Both were pure investment banks that could just as easily have been mismanaged to death before 1999. The same goes for Countrywide, Washington Mutual and Wachovia, commercial lenders that blew up without dabbling in investment banking. For another, the claim that the economic performance of the US economy before Ronald Reagan was superior to what followed because of the tighter controls on banks before 1980 is simply laughable. Productivity certainly grew faster between 1950 and 1979 than between 1980 and 2009. But it grew faster in the 1980s and 1990s than in the 1970s. And it consistently grew faster than in Canada after 1979. Unlike Paul Krugman, I think there were probably a few other factors at work in the changing productivity growth of the past seventy years: changes in technology, education and globalization are among those that spring to mind. But if I wanted to make his kind of facile argument I could triumphantly point out that Canada retained a far more tightly regulated banking system than the US – and as a result lagged behind in terms of productivity.

To a British reader, if not to an American, there is something especially implausible about the story that regulated financial markets were responsible for rapid growth, while deregulation caused crisis. British banking was also tightly regulated prior to the 1980s. The old City of London was constrained by an elaborate web of traditional guild-like restrictions. The merchant banks – members of the august Accepting Houses Committee – concerned themselves, at least notionally, with accepting commercial bills and issuing bonds and shares. Commercial or retail banking was controlled by a cartel of big 'high street' banks, which set deposit and lending rates. Within the Stock Exchange, autonomous brokers sold, while jobbers bought. Over all these gentlemanly capitalists, the Governor of the Bank of England watched with a benign but sometimes stern headmasterly eye, checking ungentlemanly conduct with a mere movement of his celebrated eyebrows.[8] On top of these conventions, a bewildering range of statutory regulations had been imposed before, during and after the Second World War. The 1947 Exchange Control Act strictly limited transactions in currencies other than sterling, controls that remained in place until 1979. Even after the breakdown of the system of fixed exchange rates established at Bretton Woods, the Bank of England routinely intervened to influence the sterling exchange rate. Banks were regulated under the 1948 Companies Act, the 1958 Prevention of Fraud (Investments) Act and the 1967 Companies Act. The 1963 Protection of Depositors Act created an additional tier of regulation for deposit-taking institutions that were not classified as banks under the arcane rules known as 'Schedule 8' and 'Section 127'.[9] Following the report of the 1959 Radcliffe Committee, which argued that the traditional tools of monetary policy were insufficient, a fresh layer of controls was added in the form of ceilings on bank lending.[10] Consumer credit (which mainly took the form of 'hire purchase' or instalment plans) was also tightly regulated. Banks recognized as such by the Old Lady of Threadneedle Street were required to maintain a 28 per cent liquidity ratio, which in practice meant holding large amounts of British government bonds.

Yet there was anything but 'spectacular economic progress' in this era of financial regulation. On the contrary, the 1970s were arguably Britain's most financially disastrous decade since the 1820s, witnessing not only a major banking crisis, but also a stock market crash, a real estate bubble and bust and double-digit inflation, all rounded off by the arrival of the International Monetary Fund in 1976. That era also had its Bernie Madoff, its Bear Stearns and its Lehman Brothers – though who now remembers Gerald Caplan of London and County Securities, or Cedar Holdings, or Triumph Investment Trust? Admittedly, the secondary banking crisis was partly due to a botched change to banking regulation by the government of Edward Heath. But it would be quite wrong to characterize this as deregulation; if anything, the new system – named, significantly, 'Competition and Credit Control' – was more elaborate than the one it replaced. Moreover, egregious errors of monetary and fiscal policy were just as important in the crisis that followed. In my view, the lesson of the 1970s is not that deregulation is bad, but that bad regulation is bad, especially in the context of bad monetary and fiscal policy.[11] And I believe the very same can be said of our crisis, too.

A Regulated Crisis

The financial crisis that began in 2007 had its origins precisely in over-complex regulation. A serious history of the crisis would need to have at least five chapters on its perverse consequences:

First, the executives of large publicly owned banks were strongly incentivized to 'maximize shareholder value' since their own wealth and income came to consist in large measure of shares and share options in their own institutions. The easiest way they could do this was to maximize the size of their banks' activities relative to their capital. All over the Western world, balance sheets grew to dizzying sizes relative to bank equity. How was this possible? The answer is that it was expressly permitted by regulation. To be precise, the Basel Committee on Banking Supervision's 1988 Accord allowed very large quantities of assets to be held by banks relative to their capital, provided these assets were classified as low risk – for example, government bonds.

Secondly, from 1996 the Basel rules were modified to allow firms effectively to set their own capital requirements on the basis of their internal risk estimates. In practice, risk weightings came to be based on the ratings given to securities – and, later, to structured financial products – by the private rating agencies.

Thirdly, central banks – led by the Federal Reserve – evolved a peculiarly lopsided doctrine of monetary policy, which taught that they should intervene by cutting interest rates if asset prices abruptly fell, but should not intervene if they rose rapidly, so long as the rise did not affect public expectations of something called 'core' inflation (which excludes changes in the prices of food and energy and wholly failed to capture the bubble in house prices). The colloquial term for this approach is the 'Greenspan (later Bernanke) put', which implied that the Fed would inter-vene to prop up the US equity market, but would not intervene to deflate an asset bubble. The Fed was sup-posed to care only about consumer-price inflation, and for some obscure reason not about house-price inflation.

Fourthly, the US Congress passed legislation designed to increase the percentage of lower-income families – espe-cially minority families – that owned their own homes. The mortgage market was highly distorted by the 'government-sponsored entities' Fannie Mae and Freddie Mac. Both parties viewed this as desirable for social and political reasons. Neither considered that, from a financial viewpoint, they were encouraging low-income households to place large, leveraged, unhedged and unidirectional bets on the US housing market.

A final layer of market distortion was provided by the Chinese government, which spent literally trillions of dollars' worth of its own currency to prevent it from appreciating relative to the dollar. The primary objective of this policy was to keep Chinese manufacturing exports ultra-competitive in Western markets. Nor were the Chinese the only ones who chose to plough their current account surpluses into dollars. The secondary and unintended consequence was to provide the United States with a vast credit line. Because much of what the surplus countries bought was US government or government agency debt, the yields on these securities were artificially held low. Because mortgage rates are closely linked to Treasury yields, 'Chimerica' – as I christened this strange economic partnership between China and America – thus helped further to inflate an already bubbling property market.

The only chapter in this history that really fits the 'blame deregulation' thesis is the non-regulation of the market in derivatives such as credit default swaps. The insurance giant AIG came to grief because its London office sold vast quantities of mispriced insurance against outcomes that properly belonged in the realm of uninsurable uncertainty. However, I do not believe this can be seen as a primary cause of the crisis. Banks were the key to the crisis, and banks were regulated.*

The issue of derivatives is important because figures as respected as Paul Volcker and Adair Turner have cast doubt on the economic and social utility of most, if not all, recent theoretical and technical advances in finance, including the advent of the derivatives market.[12] I am rather less hostile than they are to financial innovation. I agree that modern techniques of risk management were in many ways defective – especially when misused by people who forgot (or never knew) the simplifying assumptions underlying measures like Value at Risk. But modern finance cannot somehow be wished away, any more than Amazon and Google can be abolished to protect the livelihoods of booksellers and librarians.

The issue is whether or not additional regulation of the sort that is currently being devised and implemented can improve matters by reducing the frequency or magnitude of future financial crises. I think it is highly unlikely. Indeed, I would go further. I think the new regulations may have precisely the opposite effect.

The problem we are dealing with here is not inherent in financial innovation. It is inherent in financial regulation. Private sector models of risk management were undoubt-

* In the United States by (among other measures) the International Lending Supervision Act of 1983, the Financial Institutions Reform, Recovery, and Enforcement Act of 1989 and the Federal Deposit Insurance Corporation Improvement Act of 1991.

edly imperfect, as the financial crisis made clear. But public sector models of risk management were next to non-existent. Because legislators and regulators acted with an almost complete disregard for the law of unintended consequences, they inadvertently helped to inflate a real estate bubble in countries all over the developed world.[13]

The question for me is not 'Should financial markets be regulated?' There is in fact no such thing as an unregulated financial market, as any student of ancient Mesopotamia knows. The Scotland of Adam Smith had a lively debate about the kind of regulation appropriate to a paper-money system. Indeed, the founder of free-market economics himself proposed a number of quite strict bank regulations in the wake of the 1772 Ayr Banking Crisis.[14] Without rules to enforce the payment of debts and punish fraud, there can be no finance. Without restraint on the management of banks, some are very likely to fail in a downturn because of the mismatch between the durations of assets and liabilities that has been inherent in nearly all banking since the advent of the fractional reserve system. So the right question to ask is: 'What kind of financial regulation works best?'

Today, it seems to me, the balance of opinion favours complexity over simplicity; rules over discretion; codes of compliance over individual and corporate responsibility. I believe this approach is based on a flawed understanding of how financial markets work. It puts me in mind of the great Viennese satirist Karl Kraus's famous quip about psycho-analysis: that it was the disease of which it pretended to be the cure. I believe excessively complex regulation is the disease of which it pretends to be the cure.

Who Regulates the Regulators?

'We cannot control ourselves. You have to step in and control [Wall] Street.'[15] Those were the words of John Mack, former chief executive of the investment bank Morgan Stanley, speaking in New York in November 2009 (to audible gasps). Congress obliged Mr Mack by producing the Wall Street Reform and Consumer Protection Act of July 2010 (henceforth the Dodd–Frank Act, after the names of its two principal sponsors in the Senate and House, respectively).

The rule of law has many enemies. One of them is bad law. Formally intended to 'promote the financial stability of the United States by improving accountability and transparency in the financial system, to end "too big to fail" [institutions], to protect the American taxpayer by ending bailouts, to protect consumers from abusive financial services practices, and for other purposes', Dodd–Frank is a near-perfect example of excessive complexity in regulation. The Act requires that regulators create 243 rules, conduct 67 studies and issue 22 periodic reports. It eliminates one regulator and creates two new ones. It sets out detailed provisions for the 'orderly liquidation' of a Systemically Important Financial Institution (SIFI). It implements a soft version of the so-called Volcker rule, which bans SIFIs from engaging in 'proprietary trading', or sponsoring or owning interests in private equity funds and hedge funds. But that is not all.

Section 232 stipulates that each regulatory agency must establish 'an Office of Minority and Women Inclusion' to ensure, among other things, 'increased participation of minority-owned and women-owned businesses in the programs and contracts of the agency'. Unless you believe, with the head of the International Monetary Fund, Christine Lagarde, that there would have been no crisis if the best-known bank to fail had been called 'Lehman Sisters' rather than Lehman Brothers, you may well wonder what exactly this particular section of Dodd–Frank will do to 'promote the financial stability of the United States'. The same goes for Section 750, which creates a new Interagency Working Group, to 'conduct a study on the oversight of existing and prospective carbon markets to ensure an efficient, secure, and transparent carbon market', and Section 1502, which stipulates that products can be labelled as 'DRC conflict free' if they do not contain 'conflict minerals that directly or indirectly finance or benefit armed groups in the Democratic Republic of the Congo or an adjoining country'. Conflict diamonds are bad, of course, as are race and sex discrimination, not forgetting climate change. But was this really the appropriate place to deal with such things?

Title II of Dodd–Frank spends nearly eighty pages setting out in minute detail how a SIFI could be wound up with less disruption than the bankruptcy of Lehman Brothers caused. But in the final analysis what this legislation does is to transfer ultimate responsibility to the Treasury Secretary, the Federal Deposit Insurance Corporation, the District of Columbia district court and the DC court of appeals. If the Treasury Secretary and the Federal Deposit Insurance Corporation agree that a financial firm's failure could cause general instability, they can seize control of it. If the firm objects, the courts in Washington have one day to decide if the decision was correct. It is a criminal offence to disclose that such a case is being heard. How this extraordinary procedure is an improvement on a regular bankruptcy is beyond me.[16] Perhaps, on reflection, SIFI should be pronounced 'sci-fi'.

As I have suggested, it was the most-regulated institutions in the financial system that were in fact the most disaster-prone: big banks on both sides of the Atlantic, not hedge funds. It is more than a little convenient for America's political class to have the crisis blamed on deregulation and the resulting excesses of bankers. Not only does that neatly pass the buck it also creates a justification for more regulation. But the old Latin question is apposite here: *quis custodiet ipsos custodes?* Who regulates the regulators?

Now consider another set of regulations. Under the Basel III Framework for bank capital standards, which is due to come into force between 2013 and the end of 2018, the world's twenty-nine largest global banks will need to raise an additional $566 billion in new capital or shed around $5.5 trillion in assets. According to the rating agency Fitch, this implies a 23 per cent increase relative to the capital the banks had at the end of 2011.[17] It is quite true that big banks became under-capitalized – or excessively leveraged, if you prefer that term – after 1980. But it is far from clear how forcing banks to hold more capital or make fewer loans can be compatible with the goal of sustained economic recovery, without which financial stability is very unlikely to return to the US, much less in Europe.

Lurking inside every such regulation is the universal law of unintended consequences. What if the net effect of all this regulation is to make the SIFIs more rather than less systemically risky? One of many new features of Basel III is a requirement for banks to build up capital in good times, so as to have a buffer in bad times. This innovation was widely hailed some years ago when it was introduced by Spanish bank regulators. Enough said.

Unintelligent Design

In the preceding chapter, I tried to show the value of Mandeville's *Fable of the Bees* as an allegory of the way good political institutions work. Now let me introduce a different biological metaphor. In his autobiography, Charles Darwin himself explicitly acknowledged his debt to the economists of his day, notably Thomas Malthus, whose *Essay on the Principle of Population* he read 'for amusement' in 1838. 'Being well prepared', Darwin recalled, 'to appreciate the struggle for existence which everywhere goes on[,] from long-continued observation of the habits of animals and plants, it at once struck me that under these circumstances favourable variations would tend to be preserved, and unfavourable ones to be destroyed. Here, then, I had at last got a theory by which to work.'[18] The editor of the *Economist* Walter Bagehot was only one of many Victorian contemporaries who drew the parallel back from Darwin's theory of evolution to the economy. As he once observed: 'The rough and vulgar structure of English commerce is the secret of its life; for it contains the "propensity to variation", which, in the social as in the animal kingdom, is the principle of progress.'[19] We shall hear more from Bagehot below.

There are indeed more than merely superficial resemblances between a financial market and the natural world as Darwin came to understand it. Like the wild animals of the Serengeti, individuals and firms are in a constant struggle for existence, a contest over finite resources. Natural selection operates, in that any innovation (or mutation, in nature's terms) will flourish or will die depending on how well it suits its environment. What are the common features shared by the financial world and a true evolutionary system? As I have argued elsewhere,[20] there are at least six:

- 'genes', in the sense that certain features of corporate culture perform the same role as genes in biology, allowing information to be stored in the 'organizational memory' and passed on from individual to individual or from firm to firm when a new firm is created;
- the potential for spontaneous 'mutation', usually referred to in the economic world as innovation and primarily, though by no means always, technological;
- competition between individuals within a species for resources, with the outcomes in terms of longevity and proliferation determining which business practices persist;
- a mechanism for natural selection through the market allocation of capital and human resources and the possibility of death in cases of under-performance – that is, 'differential survival';
- scope for speciation, sustaining biodiversity through the creation of wholly new 'species' of financial institutions;
- scope for extinction, with certain species dying out altogether.

Sometimes, as in the natural world, the financial evolutionary process has been subject to big disruptions in the form of geopolitical shocks and financial crises. The difference is, of course, that whereas giant asteroids come from outer space, financial crises originate within the system. The Great Depression of the 1930s and the Great Inflation of the 1970s stand out as times of major discontinuity, with 'mass extinctions' such as the bank panics of the 1930s and the Savings and Loans failures of the 1980s. A comparably large disruption has clearly happened in our time. But where are the mass extinctions? The dinosaurs still roam the financial world.

The answer is that, whereas evolution in biology takes place in a pitiless natural environment, evolution in finance occurs within a regulatory framework where – to adapt a phrase from anti-Darwinian creationists – 'intelligent design' plays a part. But just how intelligent is this design? The answer is: not intelligent enough to second-guess the evolutionary process. In fact, stupid enough to make a fragile system even more fragile.

Think of it this way. The regulatory frameworks of the post-1980 period encouraged many banks to increase their balance sheets relative to their capital. This happened in all kinds of different countries, in Germany and Spain as much as in the United States. (We really cannot blame Ronald Reagan for what happened in Berlin and Madrid.) When property-backed assets fell in price, banks were threatened with insolvency. When short-term funding dried up, they were threatened with illiquidity. The authorities found that they had to choose between a Great Depression scenario of massive bank failures or bailing the banks out. They bailed them out. Chastened by ungrateful voters (who still do not appreciate how much worse things could have got if the 'too big' had actually failed), the legislators now draw up statutes designed to avoid future bail-outs.

Dodd–Frank states clearly that taxpayers will not pay a penny the next time a SIFI goes bust. It is rather less clear about who will pay. Section 214 is (mercifully) unambiguous: 'All funds expended in the liquidation of a financial company under this title shall be recovered from the disposition of assets of such financial company, or shall be the responsibility of the financial sector, through assessments.' So what about secured creditors, the bank bondholders whom so much was done to protect from loss in 2008–9? Prudently, Dodd–Frank commissions a study on that one. After all, if the net effect of the legislation really is to rule out any public funding for a seriously bankrupt SIFI, it is hard to see how those bondholders can avoid a sizeable loss. But if that is the case, then the cost of capital for big banks must rise, even as their return on equity is going down. You wanted to reduce instability, but all you did was increase fragility.

Another and related way of thinking about the financial system is as a highly complex system, made up of a very large number of interacting components that are asymmetrically organized in a network.[21] This network operates somewhere between order and disorder – on 'the edge of chaos'. Such complex systems can appear to operate quite smoothly for some time, apparently in equilibrium, in reality constantly adapting as positive feedback loops operate.

But there comes a moment when they 'go critical'. A slight perturbation can set off a 'phase transition' from a benign equilibrium to a crisis. This is especially common where the network nodes are 'tightly coupled'. When the inter-relatedness of a network increases, conflicting constraints can quickly produce a 'complexity catastrophe'.

All complex systems in the natural world – from termite hills to large forests to the human nervous system – share certain characteristics. A small input to such a system can produce huge, unanticipated changes. Causal relationships are often non-linear. Indeed, some theorists would go so far as to say that certain complex systems are wholly non-deterministic, meaning that it is next to impossible to make predictions about their future behaviour based on past data. Will the next forest fire be tiny or huge, a bonfire or a confla-gration? We can't be sure. The same 'power law' relation-ship seems to apply to earthquakes and epidemics.[22]

It turns out that financial crises are much the same. And this should not surprise us. As heterodox economists like W. Brian Arthur have been arguing for years, a complex economy is characterized by the interaction of dispersed agents, a lack of any central control, multiple levels of organ-ization, continual adaptation, incessant creation of new market niches and no general equilibrium. Viewed in this light, as Andrew Haldane of the Bank of England has argued, Wall Street and the City of London are parts of one of the most complex systems that human beings have ever made (see Figure 2.1).[23] And the combination of concentration,

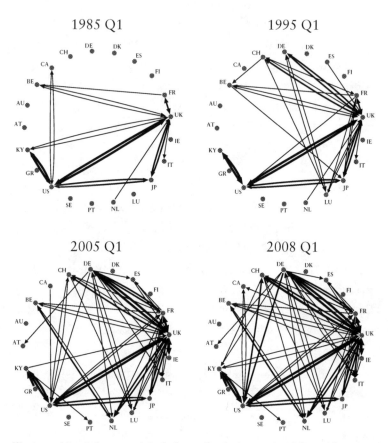

Figure 2.1 Network connectivity balloons for the international financial system
Source: Andrew Haldane, Bank of England (see note 23 for full reference).

interbank lending, financial innovation and technological acceleration makes it a system especially prone to crash. Once again, however, the difference between the natural world and the financial world is the role of regulation. Regulation is supposed to reduce the number and size of financial forest fires. And yet, as we have seen, it can quite easily have the opposite effect. This is because the political process is itself somewhat complex. Regulatory bodies can be captured by those whom they are supposed to be regulating, not least by the prospect of well-paid jobs should the gamekeeper turn poacher. They can also be captured in other ways – for example, by their reliance on the entities they regulate for the very data they need to do their work.

In his book *Antifragile*, the statistician and options trader turned philosopher Nassim Taleb asks a wonderful question: what is the opposite of fragile? The answer is not 'robust' or 'strong', because those words simply mean less fragile. The true opposite of fragile is 'anti-fragile'. A system that becomes stronger when subjected to perturbation is anti-fragile.[24] The point is that regulation should be designed to heighten anti-fragility. But the regulation we are contemplating today does the opposite: because of its very complexity – and often contradictory objectives – it is pro-fragile.

Lessons from Lombard Street

Over-complicated regulation can indeed be the disease of which it purports to be the cure. Just as the planners of the old Soviet system could never hope to direct a modern economy in all its complexity, for reasons long ago explained by Friedrich Hayek and Janos Kornai,[25] so the regulators of the post-crisis world are doomed to fail in their efforts to make the global financial system crisis-free. They can never know enough to manage such a complex system. They will only ever learn from the last crisis how to make the next one.

Is there an alternative? I believe there is. But we need to go back to the time of Darwin to find it. In *Lombard Street*, published in 1873, Walter Bagehot described with great skill the way in which the City of London had evolved in his time. Bagehot understood that, for all its Darwinian vigour, the British financial system was complex and fragile. 'In exact proportion to the power of this system', he observed, 'is its delicacy – I should hardly say too much if I said its danger . . . even at the last instant of prosperity, the whole structure is delicate. The peculiar essence of our financial system is an unprecedented trust between man and man; and when that trust is much weakened by hidden causes, a small accident may greatly hurt it, and a great accident for a moment may almost destroy it.'[26]

No one has ever given a better description of how a bank run happens than Bagehot; those unfamiliar with *Lombard Street* had to find out for themselves in 2007, at the time of the runs on Northern Rock and Countrywide, and again in 2012, when it was the turn of the Spanish Bankia to lose the confidence of its depositors. One of the great beauties of *Lombard Street* is the way it surveys all the key institutions of the London money market – the ascendant joint-stock banks, the waning private banks, the bill brokers, the new savings banks – and exposes the weakness in the position of each. In theory, Bagehot would have preferred a system in which each institution had to look to itself by maintaining a reserve against contingencies. But in practice the London market had evolved in such a way that there was only one ultimate reserve for the entire City and that was the Bank of England's: 'the sole considerable unoccupied mass of cash in the country'.[27] As in our time, in other words, the central bank (and, behind it, the government that called it into being) constituted the last line of resistance in time of panic.

By reviewing half a century of financial crises, Bagehot brilliantly showed how the Bank of England's role as custodian of the nation's cash reserve was quite different from its role as defined by statute or, indeed, as understood by the men running it. In the 1825 panic the Bank had done the right thing, but much too late in the day, and without knowing quite why it was the right thing. In each of the three panics that followed the passage of the Bank Charter Act of 1844 – a piece of legislation which was largely concerned with the Bank's note-issuing function – the Act had been suspended. There was, as in our time, uncertainty about which securities it would accept as collateral in a crisis. The Bank's governance structure was opaque. Its governor and directors were themselves not bankers. (In those days they chose merchants; nowadays we prefer academics – which not everyone would regard as an improvement.) They barely coped when a SIFI called Overend Gurney blew up in 1866.

Bagehot's remedies were clear-cut, though I believe they are very often misinterpreted. The famous recommendation was that in a crisis the central bank should lend freely at a penalty rate: 'Very large loans at very high rates are the best remedy . . .'[28] Nowadays we follow only the first half of his advice, in the belief that our system is so leveraged that high rates would kill it. Bagehot's rationale was to 'prevent the greatest number of applications by persons who do not require it'.[29] Watching all banks, strong and weak alike, gorge themselves on today's seemingly limitless supply of loans at near-zero rates, I see what he meant.

We also neglect the rest of what Bagehot said, and in particular the emphasis he laid on discretion as opposed to set rules. In the first place, he stressed the importance of having Bank directors with considerable market experience. 'Steady merchants', he wrote, 'always know the questionable standing of dangerous persons; they are quick to note the smallest signs of corrupt transactions.' Executive power should be conferred on a new, full-time deputy governor acting as a kind of permanent undersecretary. And the advisory Court should be selected so as 'to introduce . . . a wise *apprehensiveness*'.[30]

Secondly, Bagehot repeatedly stressed, as he put it, 'the cardinal importance of [the Bank of England's] always retaining a great banking reserve'. But he was emphatic that the size of the reserve should not be specified by some automatic rule, the way the banknote circulation was under the 1844 Bank Charter Act: 'No certain or fixed proportion of its liabilities can in the present times be laid down as that which the Bank ought to keep in reserve.' The ideal central bank would target nothing more precise than an 'apprehension minimum', which 'no abstract argument, and no mathematical computation will teach to us':

> And we cannot expect that they should [he went on]. Credit is an opinion generated by circumstances and varying with those circumstances. The state of credit ... can only be known by trial and inquiry. And in the same way, nothing can tell us what amount of 'reserve' will create a diffused confidence; on such a subject there is no way of arriving at a just conclusion except by incessantly watching the public mind, and seeing at each juncture how it is affected.[31]

Nor should there be predictability in the Bank's discount rate, the rate at which it lent against good-quality commercial paper. The rule 'that the Bank of England should look to the market rate and make its own rate conform to that ... was ... always erroneous', according to Bagehot. The 'first duty' of the Bank was to use the discount rate to 'protect the ultimate cash of the country'.[32] This too of course implied a discretionary power, since the desirable size of the reserve was not specified by any rule.

There are some today, like Larry Kotlikoff and John

Kay, who see the only salvation in a root-and-branch structural reform of our financial system: 'narrow banking' of some sort, if not the replacement of banks altogether.[33] I can see the intellectual appeal of such arguments. In theory, perhaps it would be much better if big banks were chopped up, leverage ratios were drastically reduced and the interconnections between deposit-takers and risk-takers were reduced.[34] But, like Bagehot, I take the world as I find it, and I do not expect to see in my lifetime a wholesale abandonment of the current model of 'too big to fail' institutions backstopped by the central bank and, if necessary, by the public purse. Our task, like Bagehot's, is 'to make the best of our banking system, and to work it in the best way that it is capable of. We can only use palliatives, and the point is to get the best palliative we can.'[35]

How to Encourage Bankers

'The problem is delicate,' as Bagehot candidly concluded his great work, and 'the solution is varying and difficult.'[36] It remains so today. But I believe a return to Bagehot's first principles would not be a bad starting point. First, strengthen the central bank as the ultimate authority in both the monetary and supervisory systems. Second, ensure that those in charge at the central bank are 'apprehensive' as well as experienced, so that they will act when they see excessive credit growth and asset-price inflation. Third, give them considerable latitude in their use of the principal central banking tools of reserve requirements, interest rate changes and open-market securities purchases and sales. Fourth, teach them some financial history, as Bagehot taught his readers.

Finally – a point Bagehot did not need to make because in his time it was a matter of course – we must ensure that those who fall foul of the regulatory authority pay dearly for their transgressions. Those who believe this crisis was caused by deregulation have misunderstood the problem in more than one way. Not only was misconceived regulation a large part of the cause. There was also the feeling of impunity that came not from deregulation but from non-punishment.

There will always be greedy people in and around banks. After all, they are where the money is – or is supposed to be. But greedy people will commit fraud or negligence only if they feel that their misdemeanour is unlikely to be noticed or severely punished. The failure to apply regulation – to apply the law – is one of the most troubling aspects of the years since 2007. In the United States, the list of those who have been sent to jail for their part in the housing bubble, and all that followed from it, is risibly short. In the United Kingdom, the harshest punishment meted out to a banker was the 'cancellation and annulment' of the former Royal Bank of Scotland CEO Fred Goodwin's knighthood.

Bagehot never got the powerful and permanent deputy governor that he proposed; instead the governor himself became both less powerful and less permanent. Since being deprived of his regulatory role, which was handed to the Financial Services Authority by Gordon Brown, the governor has been in the unenviable position of running a monetary policy research department (combined recently with an emergency money-printing works). The Federal Reserve System, too, has no real teeth. The agencies supposed to prosecute fraud have performed miserably. The result is that very few malefactors have been brought to justice in a meaningful way.

I will cite just one of many possible examples. In October 2010 Angelo Mozilo reached a settlement with the Securities and Exchange Commission in which he agreed to pay $67.5 million in penalties and 'disgorgements' to settle civil fraud and insider-trading charges relating to his time as CEO of Countrywide, the failed mortgage lender. At least part of this fine was paid not by Mozilo himself but by Bank of America, which acquired Countrywide in the depths of the financial crisis, and by insurers. Between 2000 and 2008 Mozilo received nearly $522 million in total compensation, including sales of Countrywide stock: nearly ten times more than the fine.[37] If there was nothing criminal in his conduct, it is surely only because the criminal law is defective in this area.

Voltaire famously said that the British periodically executed an admiral *pour encourager les autres*. All the detailed regulation in the world will do less to avert a future financial crisis than the clear and present danger in the minds of today's bankers that, if they transgress in the eyes of the authority on whom their business ultimately depends, then they could go to prison. Instead of exhausting ourselves drawing up hopelessly complex codes of 'macro-prudential' or 'counter-cyclical' regulation, let us go back to Bagehot's world, where individual prudence – rather than mere compliance – was the advisable course, precisely because the authorities were powerful and the crucial rules unwritten.

I began this chapter by contradicting the proponents of stricter regulation, only to end it by advocating the exemplary incarceration of bad bankers. I hope it is now clear why these positions are not contradictory but complementary. A complex financial world will be made less fragile only by simplicity of regulation and strength of enforcement.

To repeat: among the most deadly enemies of the rule of law is bad law. The next chapter will consider at a more general level the ways in which the rule of law itself, broadly defined, has degenerated in Western societies – and especially in the United States – in our time. In the realm of regulation, as I have said, we ought to be going back to Bagehot. But has the legal system in the English-speaking world inadvertently gone back to Dickens? Has the rule of law degenerated into the rule of lawyers?

3. The Landscape of Law

The Lure of Law

> The fundamental question the Chinese government must
> face is lawlessness. China does not lack laws, but the rule
> of law . . . This issue of lawlessness may be the greatest
> challenge facing the new leaders who will be installed this
> autumn [of 2012] . . . Indeed, China's political stability
> may depend on its ability to develop the rule of law in a
> system where it barely exists.[1]

These are the words of Chen Guangcheng, the blind law-
yer who was allowed to leave China to study in the United
States after successfully escaping from his Communist
Party persecutors in April 2012. Less well known in the
West, but more influential in China, is the legal scholar He
Weifang. In an essay entitled 'China's First Steps towards

Constitutionalism', published in 2003, He rather more tactfully observed: 'The Western legal landscape does make an interesting and illuminating contrast to China's legal situation, revealing many discrepancies and inconsistencies between the two . . . Although China's modern system was borrowed from the West . . . things often proceed in different ways between China and the West.'[2]

The theme of this chapter is the landscape of law. I want to ask what, if anything, developing countries like China can learn from the West about the rule of law. And I want to cast some doubt on the widespread assumption that our Western legal systems are in such good health that all the Chinese need to do is replicate our best practice – whatever that may be.

The English Way of Law

What exactly do we mean by the rule of law? In his book of that name,[3] the late Lord Chief Justice, Tom Bingham, specified seven criteria by which we should assess a legal system:

1. the law must be accessible and so far as possible intelligible, clear and predictable;

2. questions of legal right and liability should ordinarily be resolved by application of the law and not by the exercise of discretion;

3. the laws of the land should apply equally to all, save to the extent that objective differences [such as mental incapacity] justify differentiation;

4. ministers and public officers at all levels must exercise the powers conferred on them in good faith, fairly, for the purpose for which the powers were conferred, without exceeding the limits of such powers;

5. the law must afford adequate protection of fundamental human rights;

6. means must be provided for resolving, without prohibitive cost or inordinate delay, *bona fide* civil disputes which the parties themselves are unable to resolve; and

7. adjudicative procedures provided by the state should be fair.

Under heading 5, Bingham lists no fewer than fourteen different rights that the rule of law should be expected to protect: the right to life, protection from torture, protection from slavery and forced labour, the right to liberty and security, the right to a fair trial, protection from punishment without law, the right to respect for private/family life, freedom of thought/conscience/religion, freedom of expression, freedom of assembly/association, the right to marry, freedom from discrimination, protection of property and the right to education. (He might have gone further, since some countries today explicitly acknowledge rights to housing, healthcare, education and a clean environment. Why not a right to drinkable wine, too?)

In England, the rule of law in Bingham's sense of the term is the product of historical evolution. In 1215 Magna Carta established the principle that all Englishmen were equal before the law and that the Crown could not raise taxation without the consent of the Great Council, later Parliament. It was in the medieval period, too, that the writ of habeas corpus (against unlawful detention) came into use, that around 500 towns acquired charters of effective self-government and – after 1295 – that these boroughs were also represented in Parliament. From the time of Henry III until the time of James II there was a protracted tug of war between the monarch and Parliament, in which the Crown's tendency to sell off the royal demesne to finance wars steadily weakened its position. The culmination came, as we saw in Chapter 1, with the Glorious Revolution, which asserted the sovereignty of the king-in-Parliament. Also in the seventeenth century, torture was done away with; though it was not until a century later, with Somerset's Case in 1772, that slavery in England was definitively declared illegal. Throughout this period, the common law courts effectively resisted encroachments on their jurisdiction by institutions under royal control. Still, it was not until the 1701 Act of Settlement that the independence of the judiciary was assured with the advent of life appointments.

My undergraduate reading at Oxford persuaded me that the real point of English history was to establish, for the first time, three sacred principles. First, an Englishman's home is his castle. In the case of *Entick* v. *Carrington*, Lord Camden ruled against the government for raiding the home of the radical journalist John Entick. 'The great end for which men entered into society was to secure their property,' declared Camden, quoting John Locke. 'By the laws of England, every invasion of private property, be it ever so minute, is a trespass.' Secondly, do what you like as long as you do no harm. 'The privileges of thinking, saying, and doing what we please, and of growing as rich as we can, without any other restrictions, than that by all this we hurt not the public, nor one another, are the glorious privileges of liberty': that was the formulation of 'Cato' (the nom de plume of John Trenchard and Thomas Gordon), writing in the early 1720s. Third, mind your own bloody business. 'The taste for making others submit to a way of life which one thinks more useful for them than they do themselves', John Stuart Mill explained to the French liberal Alexis de Tocqueville, 'is not a common taste in England.'[4] And these pillars of the English rule of law, as A. V. Dicey had pointed out in 1885, were the products of a slow, incremental process of judicial decision-making in the common law courts, based in large measure on precedents. There were no 'grand declarations of principle', just the interplay of judicial memory and statutory innovations by Parliament.

I now realize that this was a rather naive reading of English legal history. As the greatest modern theorist of law in the English-speaking world, the late Ronald Dworkin, explained in *Law's Empire*, there really are principles underpinning the common law, even when those principles are not codified as they are in the US Constitution. 'We insist', writes Dworkin, 'that the state act on a single, coherent set of principles even when its citizens are divided about what the right principles of justice and fairness really are . . . Judges . . . decide hard cases by trying to find, in some coherent set of principles about people's rights and duties, the best constructive interpretation of the political structure and legal doctrine of their community.'[5] Behind the operation of the law lie two things: the integrity of judges and 'legislation . . . flowing from the community's present commitment to a background scheme of political morality'.[6] Questions concerning legality (or 'principle') are for judges to decide; questions of policy are matters for executive and legislature. In this legal world, the judge engages in an authentically Herculean struggle to arrive at a best fit between the rule that he eventually defines and applies in order to resolve the case before him and the general corpus of rules, legal policies and reasonable expectations. So even England's constitution-free common law is based (again in Dworkin's words) 'not only [on] the specific rules enacted in accordance with the community's accepted practices but also [on] the principles that provide the best moral justification for those enacted rules . . . [including] the rules that follow from those justifying principles, even though those further rules were never enacted'.[7]

Like democracy, the rule of law in this sense may be good in its own right. But it may also be good because of its material consequences. Few truths are today more universally acknowledged than that the rule of law – particularly insofar as it restrains the 'grabbing hand' of the rapacious state – is conducive to economic growth. According to Douglass North, 'the inability of societies to develop effective, low-cost enforcement of contracts is the most important source of both historical stagnation and contemporary underdevelopment . . .'[8] Enforcement of contracts by a third party is necessary to overcome the reluctance of private sector agents to participate in non-simultaneous economic transactions, especially over long distances in both time and space. Contract enforcement can be provided by private sector agencies such as exchanges, credit companies and arbitrators. But usually, in North's words, 'third-party enforcement [means] . . . the development of the state as a coercive force able to monitor property rights and enforce contracts effectively.'[9]

The problem is getting the state not to abuse its power – hence the need to constrain it. As Stanford's Avner Greif has argued, if public contract-enforcing institutions reveal information about the location and amount of private wealth, the state (or its functionaries) may be tempted to steal some or all of it.[10] Where states are not constrained by law, therefore, private contract-enforcing institutions are safer, like the network operated by eleventh-century Maghribi traders in the Mediterranean, which was based on their common Jewish religion and kinship ties, or the eighteenth-century Scottish diaspora, which had an almost global reach, or the South Asian traders of East Africa. We see such networks operating in many parts of the world today: think of the Chinese business communities operating outside China. Their defect, as with medieval guilds, is their tendency to raise entry barriers and establish monopolies, discouraging competition and reducing economic efficiency. That is why private contract enforcement tends to yield to public as economies become more sophisticated. But that process is dependent on constraining the state to use its power of coercion in such a way as to respect private property rights. In economics, that is the essential function of the rule of law. It is the property rights more than the human rights that are fundamental.

Law and Economics – and History

Few contributions to the literature on law and economics have had a greater impact than the argument of Andrei Shleifer and his co-authors that the common law system that evolved in the English-speaking world was superior in performing the twin roles of contract enforcement and coercion constraint to all other systems. Neither the French civil law system, originating in the Roman legal tradition, nor the German and Scandinavian legal systems, were as good, to say nothing of non-Western systems of law. What was it that made and makes common law economically better? In their seminal 1997 article, La Porta, Lopez-de-Silanes, Shleifer and Vishny argued that common law systems offer greater protection for investors and creditors. The result is that people with money are more willing to invest in, or lend to, other people's businesses. And higher levels of financial intermediation tend to correlate to higher rates of growth.[11]

In a succession of empirical studies, these and other scholars sought to demonstrate that common law countries:

1. have stronger investor protections and provide companies with better access to equity finance than civil law countries, as manifested in larger stock markets, more numerous firms and more initial public offerings;[12]
2. have better protection of outside investors relative to 'insiders', whereas French civil law countries have poorer protection;[13]
3. make it easier for new firms to enter the market, as manifested in the number of procedures,

number of days and costs of setting up a new business;[14]*

4. have more efficient (because less formalistic) courts, as measured by the time it takes to evict a non-paying tenant and to collect a debt after a cheque has bounced;[15]

5. regulate their labour markets less and therefore have higher labour-force participation and lower unemployment rates than civil law countries;[16]

6. have more extensive mandatory disclosure requirements, which again encourages investors;[17] and

7. have more efficient procedures in cases of insolvency, such as a hypothetical hotel bankruptcy.[18]

Summarizing their theory of the determining role of legal origins, the authors write:

Legal investor protection is a strong predictor of financial development . . . [as well as] government ownership of banks, the burden of entry regulations, regulation of labour markets, incidence of military conscription, and government ownership of the media . . . In all these spheres, civil law is associated with a heavier hand of

---

* Those countries that make it harder for new entities to enter the market do not reap benefits in terms of product quality. They do exhibit sharply higher levels of corruption and larger black or grey economies.

government ownership and regulation than common law . . . [These are in turn] associated with adverse impacts on markets such as greater corruption, larger unofficial economy, and higher unemployment . . . Common law is associated with lower formalism of judicial procedures . . . and greater judicial independence . . . Common law stands for the strategy of social control that seeks to support private market outcomes, whereas civil law seeks to replace such outcomes with state-desired allocations . . . Civil law is 'policy implementing', while common law is 'dispute resolving'.[19]

This brings us back to where we began, with the notion that there is greater 'flexibility of judicial decision-making under common law', because 'common law courts [can] use broad standards rather than specific rules'.[20]

Like so many arguments in social science, this theory of legal origins implies a certain version of history. Why did French law end up being worse than English? Because the medieval French Crown was more assertive of its prerogatives than the English. Because France was less peaceable internally and more vulnerable externally than England. Because the French Revolution, which distrusted judges, sought to convert them into automata, implementing the law as defined and codified by the legislature. The result was an even less independent judiciary and courts precluded from reviewing administrative acts. The Gallic conception of freedom was more absolute in theory and less effectual in practice. In any case, as Alexis de Tocqueville shrewdly observed when comparing the United States and France in the 1830s and 1840s, the French preferred equality to liberty. This preference resulted in a strong central state and weak civil society. When the French exported their model to their colonies in Asia and Africa, the results were even worse.

The theory of legal origins also has important historical implications for non-Western legal systems. We have already encountered Timur Kuran's argument about the retarding effects of Islamic law on Ottoman economic development. A similar case can be made for China. As He Weifang has argued, in the imperial era Chinese government made 'no arrangement whatsoever for the separation of powers', so 'the country magistrate exercised comprehensive responsibilities [including all] three basic functions, namely the enacting of rules . . . the execution of rules . . . and the resolving of disputes.' Confucianism and Taoism deprecated lawyers and deplored the adversarial mode. Yan Fu, the Chinese translator of Montesquieu, fully understood the difference between the Chinese and the Western spirit of the laws. 'During my visit to Europe [in the late 1870s],' he wrote, 'I once attended court hearings and when I came back, I felt at a loss. On one occasion, I said to Mr. Guo Songtao [the Qing ambassador to Great Britain] that, of the many reasons that make England and other European nations rich and strong, the most important one is the guarantee there of having justice done. And my view was shared by Mr. Guo.'[21]

Yet attempts to import elements of the British legal system to China were a failure. Although the imperial Chinese state sought to provide all kinds of public goods, such as defence, famine relief, commercial infrastructure like canals and the distribution of agricultural knowledge, its highly centralized bureaucracy was quite skeletal in relation to the population. Property rights were relatively secure insofar as there was little variation over time in (by Western standards) low rates of taxation, but there was no commercial code of law and magistrates were steeped in literary and philosophical learning, not in law. They sought 'compromises rather than legal rulings', leaving contract enforcement to private networks. When the late Qing state belatedly entered the commercial sphere, it did so in a counter-productive way, over-taxing merchants and delegating power to monopolistic guilds without effectively constraining itself or its agents. The results were rampant corruption and economic contraction.[22]

Law and the Victorians

The legal-origins hypothesis is not without its critics. After all, it is hard not to overlook the fact that for much of the modern era France has had a successful economy, including a large financial sector, despite not being blessed with the common law.[23] Similar things have been said about Germany and Brazil.[24] Another line of argument is that common law systems compare less favourably with civil law systems when measures of social welfare – such as infant mortality or inequality – are the dependent varia-bles.[25] Yet for me the theory's weakest point becomes apparent if we look at the state of the English common law as it was in the period when, by implication, it must have done the greatest good: the period of the Industrial Revolution, when the English and their Celtic neighbours radically altered the course of world economic history. Here is a contemporary description of an English court at that time:

> some score of members of the ... bar ... are ... mistily engaged in one of the ten thousand stages of an endless cause, tripping one another up on slippery precedents, groping knee-deep in technicalities, running their goat-hair and horsehair warded heads against walls of words and making a pretence of equity with serious faces, as players might ... the various solicitors in the cause, some two or three of whom have inherited it from their fathers, who made a fortune by it ... are ... ranged in a line, in a long matted well ... between the registrar's red table and the silk gowns, with bills, cross-bills, answers, rejoinders, injunctions, affidavits, issues, references to masters, mas-ters' reports, mountains of costly nonsense, piled before them ... This is the Court of Chancery ... which so

exhausts finances, patience, courage, hope, so overthrows the brain and breaks the heart, that there is not an honourable man among its practitioners who would not give – who does not often give – the warning, 'Suffer any wrong that can be done you rather than come here!'[26]

It might be objected that Charles Dickens was not being entirely fair to the legal profession of his day in *Bleak House*. Yet Dickens had started his career writing court reports. He had seen his own father imprisoned for debt. His biographers confirm that he knew whereof he spoke.[27] And historians of the nineteenth-century English legal system largely confirm his account.

First, we must note the tiny size of the system. As late as 1854, the entire judiciary of England and Wales sitting in courts of general jurisdiction numbered just fifteen. These judges, distributed equally between three benches, sat individually to hear cases, either in London or at assize (sessions held in major provincial towns), for just two four-week terms a year. These same men convened as panels of three or four to hear appeals and then sat in larger panels (usually numbering seven) to hear appeals from the panels of three or four. Only appeals from the panels of seven would be heard by another institution, which was the House of Lords. True, the activity of the lower county courts increased as economic life gathered pace. But that was not true of the higher courts.[28]

Second, until 1855 there were severe statutory restrictions

on the ability of entrepreneurs to create limited-liability companies, a legacy of the time when the promoters of monopoly firms like the South Sea Company had successfully pulled up the ladder behind themselves to boost the value of their own shares. As late as the 1880s, there were still only sixty domestic companies listed on the London Stock Exchange. So much for the benefits of common law for financial development. Third, in the single most important sector of the Victorian Industrial Revolution, the railways, modern research has revealed that 'English common law and common law lawyers had a profound and largely negative impact.' Solicitors were notorious as speculative railway-share promoters, judges were publicly accused of favouritism and the Parliamentary Bar ran a nice little racket, effectively selling statutory approval for new railway lines.[29]

What are we to make of this? Does history essentially refute the legal-origins thesis that the common law trumps all other systems? Not quite. For despite the evident shortcomings of the English legal system in the industrial age, there remains compelling evidence that it could and did adapt to the changes of the time, perhaps even in ways that facilitated the process as well as accommodating it. This point is best illustrated with reference to the 1854 Exchequer case (well known to law students on both sides of the Atlantic) of *Hadley* v. *Baxendale*. The dispute was between two Gloucester flour-millers, Joseph and Jonah Hadley, and Joseph Baxendale, the managing director of the London-based carriers Pickford & Co. The Hadleys had sued Pickfords for the full amount of their losses – including forgone profits – resulting from late delivery of a replacement hand-crafted mill shaft. It is no coincidence that Pickfords are still around today and the Hadleys' firm, City Flour Mills, is not. For although the local jury decided for the Hadleys, the appellate judges in London reversed their decision. According to the American judge and legal scholar Richard Posner, *Hadley* v. *Baxendale* enshrined the principle 'that where a risk of loss is known to only one party to the contract, the other party is not liable for the loss if it occur'.[30]

It was later said of the original assize judge, Sir Roger Crompton, that he 'never recognized the notion that the common law adapts itself by a perpetual process of growth to the perpetual roll of the tide of circumstances as society advances'.[31] That was certainly not the approach of the appeal judges, Barons Alderson, Parke and Martin, who – in the words of a modern commentator – 'refashioned the substantive law of contract damages'. As Alderson reasoned, 'the only circumstances . . . communicated by the plaintiffs to the defendants' at the time the contract was made were that they were millers whose mill shaft was broken. There was no notice of the 'special circumstances' that the mill was stopped and profits would be lost as a result of delay in the delivery of the shaft. Moreover, it was 'obvious [thus Alderson] that in the great multitude of cases of millers sending off broken shafts to third persons by a carrier under ordinary circumstances', the mills would not be idle and profits lost during the period of shipment, since most millers would have spare shafts.[32] Thus the loss of profits could not be taken into consideration in estimating damages.

To put it crudely, this was a ruling that favoured big over small business – but that is not really the important point. The point is that Baron Alderson's reasoning illustrates very well how the common law evolves, a process elegantly described by Lord Goff in the 1999 case of *Kleinwort Benson* v. *Lincoln City Council*:

> When a judge decides a case which comes before him, he does so on the basis of what he understands the law to be. This he discovers from the applicable statutes, if any, and from precedents drawn from reports of previous judicial decisions . . . In the course of deciding the case before him he may, on occasion, develop the common law in the perceived interests of justice, though as a general rule he does this 'only interstitially' . . . This means not only that he must act within the confines of the doctrine of precedent, but that the change so made must be seen as a development, usually a very modest development, of existing principle and so can take its place as a congruent part of the common law as a whole. In this process, what [F. W.] Maitland has called the 'seamless web', and I myself . . . have called the 'mosaic', of the common law, is kept in a constant state of adaptation and

repair, the doctrine of precedent, the 'cement of legal principle', providing the necessary stability.[33]

I believe this gives an invaluable insight into the authentically evolutionary character of the common law system.* It was this, rather than any specific functional difference in the treatment of investors or creditors, that gave the English system and its relatives around the world an advantage in terms of economic development.

The Rule of Law's Enemies

That was then. What about now? How good in practice is the rule of law in the West – and in particular in the English-speaking world – today? There are four distinct threats to it that I would identify.

First, we must pose the familiar question about how far our civil liberties have been eroded by the national security state – a process that in fact dates back almost a hundred years to the outbreak of the First World War and the passage in the UK of the 1914 Defence of the Realm Act.

---

* In our ongoing work on 'The Spirit of the Common Law', Charles Béar QC and I seek to explore in detail how precisely this evolution has worked, looking at the changing meaning of legal concepts over time rather than approaching the law in the functionalist, present-minded spirit of Shleifer *et al.*

The debates after September 11, 2001, about the protracted detention of terrorist suspects were in no way new. Somehow it is always a choice between habeas corpus and hundreds of corpses.

A second threat is the very obvious one posed by the intrusion of European law – with its civil law character – into the English legal system, in particular the far-reaching effects of the incorporation into English law of the 1953 European Convention on Fundamental Rights and Freedoms. This may be considered Napoleon's revenge: a creeping 'Frenchification' of the common law.

A third threat is the growing complexity (and sloppiness) of statute law, a grave problem on both sides of the Atlantic as the mania for elaborate regulation spreads through the political class. I agree with the American legal critic Philip K. Howard that we need a 'legal spring cleaning' of obsolete legislation and routine inclusion of 'sunset provisions' (expiry dates) in new laws.[34] We must also seek to persuade legislators that their role is not to write an 'instruction manual' for the economy that covers every eventuality, right down to the remotest imaginable risk to our health and safety.[35]

A fourth threat – especially apparent in the United States – is the mounting cost of the law. By this I do not mean the $94.5 billion a year that the US federal government spends on law making, law interpretation and law enforcement.[36] Nor do I mean the spiralling cost of lobbying by businesses seeking to protect themselves or hurt their competitors by skewing legislation in their favour. The $3.3 billion cost of paying nearly 13,000 lobbyists is in fact rather small in itself.[37] It is the cost of the consequences of their work that is truly alarming: an estimated $1.75 trillion a year, according to a report commissioned by the US Small Business Administration, in additional business costs arising from compliance with regulations.[38] On top of that are the $865 billion in costs arising from the US system of tort law, which gives litigants far greater opportunities than in England to seek damages for any 'wrongful act, damage, or injury done wilfully, negligently, or in circumstances involving strict liability, but not involving breach of contract, for which a civil suit can be brought'. According to the Pacific Research Institute's study *Jackpot Justice*, the tort system costs a sum 'equivalent to an eight per cent tax on consumption [or] a thirteen per cent tax on wages'.[39] The direct costs arising from a staggering 7,800 new cases a day were equivalent to more than 2.2 per cent of US GDP in 2003, double the equivalent figure for any other developed economy, with the exception of Italy.[40] One may argue about such figures, and of course spokesmen for the legal interest reject them.[41] But my own personal experience tells a similar story: merely setting up a new business in New England involved significantly more lawyers and much more in legal fees than doing so in England.

In their new book on the lessons for China of US legal experience, David Kennedy and Joseph Stiglitz cite three egregious defects of the rule of law in the United States today:

1. Current 'laws allowing financial firms to engage in predatory lending, combined with new bank-ruptcy laws, have created a new class of partially indentured servants – people who might have to give as much as 25 per cent of what they earn for the rest of their lives to the banks'.

2. Intellectual property laws are excessively restric-tive. For example, 'the "owner" of the patent on the gene that indicates a strong likelihood of breast cancer [could] insist on a large payment for every test performed. The resulting . . . fee puts the test out of the range of most without health insurance.'

3. 'Under current laws concerning toxic wastes . . . litigation costs represent more than a quarter of the amount spent on clean-up.'[42]

For Stiglitz, these illustrate the inadequacy of a narrow approach to law that simply assigns property rights and leaves markets to do the rest. My view is that such examples need to be seen in the wider context of over-complex or rigged legislation and rampant tort abuse.

Experts on economic competitiveness, like Michael Por-ter of Harvard Business School, define the term to include the ability of the government to pass effective laws; the protection of physical and intellectual property rights and lack of corruption; the efficiency of the legal framework, including modest costs and swift adjudication; the ease of setting up new businesses; and effective and predictable regulations.[43] It is startling to find how poorly the United States now fares when judged by these criteria. In a 2011 survey, Porter and his colleagues asked HBS alumni about 607 instances of decisions on whether or not to offshore operations. The United States retained the business in just ninety-six cases (16 per cent) and lost it in all the rest. Asked why they favoured foreign locations, the respondents listed the areas where they saw the US falling further behind the rest of the world. The top ten reasons included:

1. the effectiveness of the political system;
2. the complexity of the tax code;
3. regulation;
4. the efficiency of the legal framework;
5. flexibility in hiring and firing.[44]

Evidence that the United States is suffering some kind of institutional loss of competitiveness can be found not only in Porter's work but also in the World Economic Forum's annual Global Competitiveness Index and, in particular, the Executive Opinion Survey on which it is partly based. The survey includes fifteen measures of the rule of law, ranging from the protection of private property rights to the policing of corruption and the control of organized crime. It is an astonishing yet scarcely acknowledged fact that on no fewer than fifteen out of fifteen counts, the United States now fares markedly worse than Hong Kong. Taiwan outranks the US in nine out of fifteen. Even mainland China does better in two dimensions. Indeed, the United States makes the global top twenty in only one area. On every other count, its reputation is shockingly bad.[45] In the Heritage Foundation's Freedom Index, too, the US ranks twenty-first in the world in terms of freedom from corruption, a considerable distance behind Hong Kong and Singapore.[46]

Admittedly, these studies are based in large measure on survey data. They are subjective. Yet similar conclusions may be reached from other research based on more objective criteria, like the International Finance Corporation's data on the ease of doing business. In terms of the ease of paying taxes, for example, the United States ranks seventy-second in the world. In terms of dealing with construction permits, it ranks seventeenth; registering a property sixteenth; resolving insolvency fifteenth; and starting a business thirteenth.[47] The World Justice Project's Rule of Law 2011 index ranks the United States twenty-first out of sixty-six in terms of access to civil justice; twentieth for the effectiveness of criminal justice; nineteenth for fundamental rights; seventeenth for absence of corruption; sixteenth for the limiting of government powers; fifteenth for regulatory enforcement; thirteenth for order and security; and twelfth for the openness of government.[48]

Perhaps the most compelling evidence of all comes

from the World Bank's indicators on World Governance, which suggest that since 1996 the United States has suffered a decline in the quality of its governance in four different dimensions: government accountability and effectiveness, regulatory quality and control of corruption (see Figure 3.1).[49] Compared with Germany and Hong Kong, the US is manifestly slipping behind. This is a remarkable phenomenon in itself. Even more remarkable is that it is happening almost unnoticed by Americans. One small consolation is that the United Kingdom does not appear to have suffered a comparable decline in institutional quality.

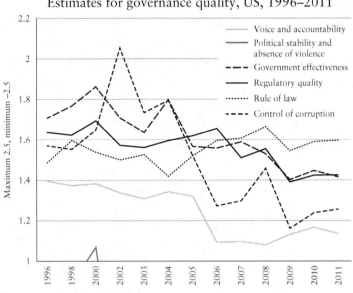

Estimates for governance quality, US, 1996–2011

Figure 3.1
Source: www.govindicators.org.

Legal Reform around the World

If the rule of law, broadly defined, is deteriorating in the United States, where is it getting better? I have already mentioned the marked improvement in institutional quality in Hong Kong. This is by no means a solitary case. All over the developing world, countries are seizing the opportunity to improve their chances of attracting foreign and domestic investment and raising the growth rate by reforming their legal and administrative systems. The World Bank now does a very good job of keeping tabs on the progress of such reforms. I recently delved into the Bank's treasure trove, the World Development Indicators database, to see which countries in Africa are ranked highly in terms of:

1. the quality of public administration;
2. the business regulatory environment;
3. property rights and rule-based governance;
4. public sector management and institutions; and
5. transparency, accountability and corruption in the public sector.

The countries that appear in the top twenty developing economies in four or more of these categories are Burkino Faso, Ghana, Malawi and Rwanda.

Another approach I have taken is to look at the IFC's *Doing Business* reports since 2006 to see which developing countries have seen the biggest reduction in the number of days it takes to complete seven procedures: starting a business, getting a construction permit, registering a property, paying taxes, importing goods, exporting and enforcing contracts.[50] The African winners are, in order of achievement, Rwanda, Nigeria, the Gambia, Mauritius and Botswana. Other emerging markets apparently on the right track are Belarus, Croatia, Georgia, Malaysia, Bosnia and Macedonia (see Figure 3.2).*

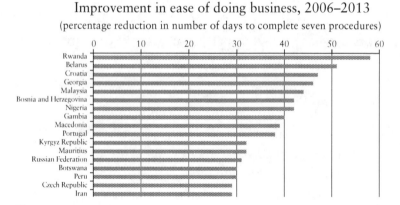

Improvement in ease of doing business, 2006–2013

(percentage reduction in number of days to complete seven procedures)

Figure 3.2
Source: International Finance Corporation, *Doing Business* reports.

* The appearance of Belarus on the list is a reminder, of course, that such datasets must be used with caution.

Development economists like Paul Collier see the establishment of the rule of law in a poor country as occurring in four distinct stages. The first and indispensable step is to reduce violence. The second is to protect property rights. The third is to impose institutional checks on government. The fourth is to prevent corruption in the public sector.[51] Interestingly, this sounds very much like a potted version of the history of England from the end of the Civil War, through the Glorious Revolution to the nineteenth century Northcote–Trevelyan reforms of the civil service.

By contrast, the People's Republic of China has achieved astonishing growth without good legal institutions and without much improvement in them. Followers of the new institutional economics have struggled to explain this seeming exception to their rule. Is it because the Communist Party somehow makes 'credible commitments' now that growth is the sole basis of its legitimacy? Is it because there are in fact 'de facto property rights'? Is it because competition between the provinces has resulted in a kind of 'market-preserving federalism'? Or is it because contracts in China are relational, not legal: in other words, contract enforcement is informal, via *guanxi* (connections or influence), rather than formal, through the law?[52] Whatever the explanation, many scholars – notably Daron Acemoglu and James Robinson – argue that if China does not now transition to the rule of law, there will be a low institutional ceiling limiting its future growth.[53] This is also the view of many Chinese legal activists, including (as we have already seen) Chen Guangcheng. And they are right.

According to one study, the average rate for enforcing civil and economic judgments in China in the mid-1990s was 60 per cent at the basic-level court, 50 per cent at the intermediate-level court, and 40 per cent at the provincial higher-level court, meaning that roughly half of Chinese court rulings at that time existed only on paper. The sort of contractual dispute that is most likely to involve significant amounts of unpaid debt – disputes involving banks and state-owned enterprises – had an average enforcement rate of just 12 per cent, even according to official estimates.[54] The case of Bo Xilai's anti-corruption campaign in Chongqing illustrates how far China still is from the rule of law. As He Weifang has pointed out, the Chongqing judges essentially acted as an arm of Bo's regime, accepting extorted confessions and omitting cross-examination. For years, He Weifang has campaigned for judicial independence, the accountability of the National People's Congress, especially with regard to taxation, the freedom of the press and the conversion of the Communist Party into a 'properly registered legal entity', subject to the law – including the currently meaningless individual rights in Article 35 of the Constitution of the People's Republic, which include freedom of association, of procession and demonstration and of religious belief. He also favours the privatization of state-owned enterprises because, as he puts it, 'private ownership is the foundation of the civil law'. Like Chen Guangcheng, he believes that the rule of law is the only way for China to escape from its historical oscillation between order and *dong luan* – turmoil.[55]

For those of us who live in the West, where lawyers often seem to have become their own vested interest, it is strange to encounter lawyers who aim at this kind of radical change. Today, however, Chinese lawyers – who numbered just 150,000 in 2007 – are a crucial force in China's rapidly evolving public sphere. Surveys suggest that they are 'strongly inclined towards political reform . . . and are profoundly discontented with the political status quo' – though this reflects not only the government interference they regularly have to endure but also the economic insecurity they suffer. Still, to read statements like the following, from a lawyer in Henan province, is to be reminded forcibly of a time when lawyers were in the vanguard of change in the English-speaking world (including in South Asian anti-colonial movements): 'The rule of law is premised on democracy; rights are premised on the rule of law; rights defence is premised on rights; and lawyers are premised on rights defence.'[56]

The fall of Bo Xilai in 2012 is one of a number of signs that elements within the Communist Party hear these arguments. In a speech in Shenzhen in June that year, Zhang Yansheng, secretary general of the academic committee for National Development and Reform, argued that 'we should shift towards reform based on rules and law,' adding: 'If such reform does not take off, China will run into big trouble, big problems.'[57] What we do not know is whether or not China's next experiment with importing the essentially Western notion of the rule of law will be more successful than past attempts. With good reason, He Weifang warns against naive imitation of the English (or American) legal system. 'In Shakespeare's *A Midsummer Night's Dream*,' he writes in an engaging aside, 'a person was changed into a donkey, and the other person cried, "Bless thee! Thou art translated!" The introduction of a Western system to China is just like this.' Common law translated into Chinese might well turn out to be like Bottom: a donkey, if not an ass.[58]

The Rule of Lawyers

Like the human hive of politics or the hunting grounds of the market economy, the legal landscape is an integral part of the institutional setting in which we live our lives. Like a true landscape, it is organic, the product of slow-moving historical processes – a kind of judicial geology. But it is also a landscape in the sense of 'Capability' Brown: it can be improved upon. And it can also be made hideous – even rendered a desert – by the rash imposition of utopian designs. Oriental gardens flourish in England and English gardens in the Orient. But there are limits to what transplantation can achieve.

Once-verdant landscapes can become desiccated through natural processes, too. Mancur Olson used to argue that, over time, all political systems are likely to succumb to sclerosis, mainly because of rent-seeking activities by organized interest groups.[59] Perhaps that is what we see at work in the United States today. Americans could once boast proudly that their system set the benchmark for the world; the United States *was* the rule of law. But now what we see is the rule of *lawyers*, which is something different. It is surely no coincidence that lawyers are so over-represented in the US Congress. The share of senators who are lawyers is admittedly below its peak of 51 per cent in the early 1970s but it is still 37 per cent. Similarly, lawyers no longer account for 43 per cent of representatives in the House, as in the early 1960s, but at 24 per cent their share is still much larger than the equivalent figure for the House of Commons (14 per cent).[60]

Olson also argued that it can require an external shock – like a lost war – to sweep away the stifling residues of cronyism and corruption, and allow the rule of law in Bingham's and Dworkin's senses of the term to be re-established. It must fervently be hoped that the United States can avoid such a painful form of therapy. But how is the system to be reformed if, as I have argued, there is so much that is rotten within it: in the legislature, in the regulatory agencies, in the legal system itself?

The answer, as I shall argue in the next and final chapter, is that reform – whether in the English-speaking world or the Chinese-speaking – must come from outside the realm of public institutions. It must come from the associations of civil society. It must come, in short, from us: the citizens.

4. Civil and Uncivil Societies

Clearing the Beach

Nearly ten years ago I bought a house on the coast of South Wales. With its rugged, windswept Atlantic coastline, its rain-soaked golf courses, its remnants of industrial greatness and its green hills just visible through the drizzle, it reminded me a lot of where I grew up, in the West of Scotland: only slightly warmer, nearer Heathrow airport and with a rugby team more likely to beat England.

I bought the house mainly to be beside the sea. But there was a catch. The lovely stretch of coastline in front of it was hideously strewn with rubbish. Thousands of plastic bottles littered the sands and rocks. Plastic bags fluttered in the wind, caught on the thorns of the wild Burnet roses. Beer and soft-drink cans lay rusting in the dunes. Crisp packets floated in the waves like repulsive opaque jellyfish.

Where did it all come from? Some of it was clearly

dropped by local youths, who seemed indifferent to the ruinous effect of their behaviour on the natural beauty of the land of their fathers. But much more seemed to come in from the sea. I began to read, with mounting horror, about the extent of offshore refuse dumping. It is a practice beyond the control of any government, regulator or law. Unlike a landfill site, the ocean is a free rubbish dump. Unlike the stuff earlier generations threw into it, plastic rubbish is neither biodegradable nor heavy enough to sink. Where it ends up is decided by the currents, tides and winds. Unfortunately for me, those of the Bristol Channel seemed intent on depositing a disproportionate share of all the trash in the North Atlantic in my backyard.

Dismayed, I asked the locals who was responsible for keeping the coastline clean. 'The council is supposed to do it, down by here,' one of them explained. 'But they don't do nothing about it, do they?' This was not so much *Under Milk Wood* as *Under Milk Carton*. Infuriated, and perhaps evincing the first symptoms of an obsessive–compulsive disorder, I took to carrying and filling black bin-liners whenever I went for a walk. But it was a task far beyond the capacity of one man.

And that was when it happened. I asked for volunteers. The proposition was simple: come and help make this place look as it should; lunch provided. The first beach clear-up was a modest affair: no more than eight or nine people came, and not all of them stuck at the work, which involved backache and dirty fingers. The second was more of a success. The sun actually shone, as it sometimes – very occasionally – does.

It was when the local branch of the Lions Club got involved, however, that the breakthrough came. I had never heard of the Lions Club. I learned that it was originally an American association, not unlike the Rotary Club: both were founded by Chicago businessmen about a century ago, and both are secular networks whose members dedicate time to various good causes. The Lions brought a level of organization and motivation that far exceeded my earlier improvised efforts. As a result of their involvement, the shoreline was transformed. The plastic bottles were bagged and properly disposed of. The roses were freed from their ragged polythene wrappings. One measure of our success was a marked increase in the number of locals and visitors walking along the coastal path.

My Welsh experience taught me the power of the voluntary association as an institution. Together, spontaneously, without any public sector involvement, without any profit motive, without any legal obligation or power, we had turned a depressing dumping ground back into a beauty spot. And every time I wander down for a swim, I ask myself: how many other problems could be solved in this simple and yet satisfying way?

In the previous chapters, I have tried to prise open some tightly shut black boxes: the one labelled 'democracy', the one labelled 'capitalism' and the one labelled 'the rule of law'. In this final chapter, I want to unlock the black box labelled 'civil society'. I want to ask how far it is possible for a truly free nation to flourish in the absence of the kind of vibrant civil society we used to take for granted. I want to suggest that the opposite of civil society is uncivil society, where even the problem of anti-social behaviour becomes a problem for the state. And I want to cast doubt on the idea that the new social networks of the internet are in any sense a substitute for real networks of the sort that helped me clear my local beach.

The Rise and Fall of Social Capital

'America is, among the countries of the world,' declared Alexis de Tocqueville in the first book of his *Democracy in America*:

> the one where they have taken most advantage of association and where they have applied that powerful mode of action to a greater diversity of objects.
>
> Independent of the permanent associations created by law under the names of townships, cities and counties, there is a multitude of others that owe their birth and development only to individual will.
>
> The inhabitant of the United States learns from birth that he must rely on himself to struggle against the evils

and obstacles of life; he has only a defiant and restive regard for social authority and he appeals to its authority only when he cannot do without it ... In the United States, they associate for the goals of public security, of commerce and industry, of morality and religion. There is nothing the human will despairs of attaining by the free action of the collective power of individuals.[1]

Tocqueville saw America's political associations as an indispensable counterweight to the tyranny of the majority in modern democracy. But it was the non-political associations that really fascinated him:

Americans of all ages, all conditions, all minds constantly unite. Not only do they have commercial and industrial associations in which all take part, but they also have a thousand other kinds: religious, moral, grave, futile, very general and very particular, immense and very small; Americans use associations to give fêtes, to found seminaries, to build inns, to raise churches, to distribute books, to send missionaries to the antipodes; in this manner they create hospitals, prisons, schools. Finally, if it is a question of bringing to light a truth or developing a sentiment with the support of a great example, they associate.[2]

This is a justly famous passage, as is Tocqueville's amusing contrast between the way American citizens banded together to campaign against alcohol abuse and the approach to social problems in his native land: 'if those hundred thousand [members of the American Temperance Society] had lived in France, each of them would have addressed himself individually to the government,' begging it to oversee the nation's wine bars.[3]

Tocqueville did not exaggerate nineteenth-century America's love of voluntary associations. To give just a single example, from the historian Marvin Olasky, the associations affiliated with 112 Protestant churches in Manhattan and the Bronx at the turn of the twentieth century were responsible for forty-eight industrial schools, forty-five libraries or reading rooms, forty-four sewing schools, forty kindergartens, twenty-nine savings banks and loan associations, twenty-one employment offices, twenty gymnasia and swimming pools, eight medical dispensaries, seven full-day nurseries and four lodging houses. And this list excludes the activities of Roman Catholic, Jewish and secular voluntary associations, of which there were also plenty.[4] Continental Europe, as Tocqueville rightly noted, was never like this. In his book *The Moral Basis of a Backward Society*, Edward Banfield contrasted the 'amoral familism' of a southern Italian town he called 'Montegrano' with the rich associational life of St George, Utah. Same terrain, same climate – different institutions. In Montegrano, there was just one association: a card-playing club to which twenty-five upper-class men belonged. There was also an orphanage, run by an order of nuns in an ancient monastery, but the local townspeople did nothing to assist their efforts or help maintain the crumbling cloister.[5]

Yet, just as Tocqueville had feared, the associational vitality of the early United States has since significantly diminished. In his best-selling book *Bowling Alone*, Robert Putnam detailed the drastic declines, between around 1960 or 1970 and the late 1990s, in a long list of indicators of 'social capital':

– attendance at a public meeting on town or school affairs: down 35 per cent;
– service as an officer of a club or organization: down 42 per cent;
– service on a committee for a local organization: down 39 per cent;
– membership of parent–teacher associations: down 61 per cent;
– the average membership rate for thirty-two national chapter-based associations: down almost 50 per cent; and
– membership rates for men's bowling leagues: down 73 per cent.[6]

As Theda Skocpol argued in her 2003 study *Diminished Democracy*, organizations like the Elks, the Moose, the Rotarians and indeed my friends the Lions – which once did so much to bring together Americans of different income groups and classes – are in decline in the United States.[7] In a similar vein (though from a very different ideological point of origin), Charles Murray's superb 2012 book *Coming Apart* makes the argument that the breakdown of both religious and secular associational life in working-class communities is one of the key drivers of social immobility and widening inequality in the United States today.[8]

If the decline of American civil society is so far advanced, what hope is there for Europeans? Britain has sometimes been represented as the exception to Putnam's 'law' of declining social capital. Like the United States, the United Kingdom experienced a golden age of associational life in the nineteenth century, 'the age [in the historian G. M. Trevelyan's words] of Trade Unions, Cooperative and Benefit Societies, Leagues, Boards, Commissions, Committees for every conceivable purpose of philanthropy and culture'. As Trevelyan joked, 'not even the dumb animals were left unorganized'.[9] In 1911 the gross annual receipts of registered charities exceeded national public expenditure on the Poor Law.[10] The absolute number of cases of hardship reviewed by charities was remarkably constant between 1871 and 1945.[11] The implementation of William Beveridge's recommendation for a centrally administered system of national insurance and healthcare radically altered the role of many British 'friendly societies', either turning them into agencies of government welfare or rendering them obsolete.[12] But in other ways British associational life remained vital. In the 1950s sociologists were still impressed by the resilience of this network of voluntary societies. Indeed, according to Peter Hall, it largely survived even the 1980s, the sole exceptions being traditional women's organizations, some youth organizations and service organizations like the Red Cross, which did suffer declines of membership.[13]

However, on closer inspection, this story of resilience looks questionable. The reports of the Registrar of Friendly Societies, which began in 1875 and continued until 2001, allow us to trace over the long run the number and membership of friendly societies (such as working men's clubs), industrial and provident societies (such as co-operatives) and building societies (mutually owned saving and mortgage-lending associations). In absolute terms, the peak in the number of such societies was in 1914 (36,010) and the peak in membership in 1908 (33.8 million) – at a time when the population of the United Kingdom was just over 44 million. By contrast, there were just over 12,000 societies in 2001. Membership figures for that year are available only for the 9,000 industrial and provident societies and amount to 10.5 million, compared with a total population of 59.7 million.[14] The Manchester Unity of Oddfellows, an umbrella organization for friendly societies, had 713,000 members in 1899, compared with 230,000 today.[15] Moreover, a comparative study based on the World Values Survey showed Britain slipping from ninth to twelfth place in the international league table for voluntarism, as the share of the population claiming to be members of one or more voluntary associations fell from 52 per cent in 1981 to 43 per cent in 1991.[16] The most recent survey data indicates a further decline (see Figure 4.1) and indeed suggests that even more Britons than Americans are now 'bowling alone'.

The decline of British 'social capital' has manifestly accelerated. Not only has membership of political parties

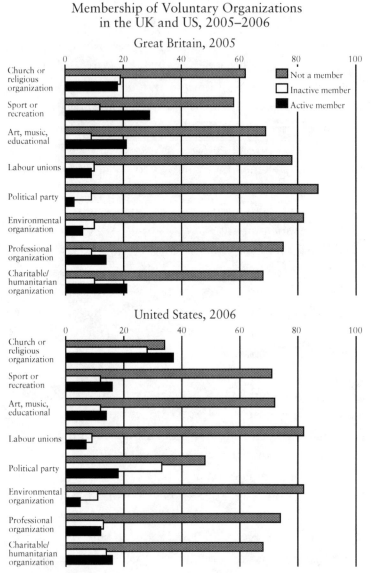

Figure 4.1 Membership of voluntary organizations in the UK and US, 2005–2006

Source: World Values Survey Association, World Value Survey, 1981–2008, official aggregate v.20090902 (2009): http://www.wvsevsdb.com/wvs/WVSIntegratedEVSWVSvariables.jsp?Idioma=I.

and trade unions plummeted, long-established charities have seen 'a marked drop in numbers'. Membership of any type of organization was also lower in 2007 than in 1997. Remarkably, according to the National Council of Voluntary Organizations, just '8 per cent of the population [accounts] for almost half of all volunteer hours'.[17] Charitable donations show a similar trend. Although the average donation has gone up, the percentage of households giving to charity has fallen since 1978 and more than a third of donations now come from the over-sixty-fives, compared with less than a quarter some thirty years ago. (In the same period, the elderly have gone from 14 per cent to 17 per cent of the population.)[18] The final publications of the Citizenship Survey for England made for truly dismal reading.[19] In 2009–10:

- Only one in ten people had any involvement in decision-making about local services or in the provision of these services (for example, being a school governor or a magistrate).
- Only a quarter of people participated in any kind of formal volunteering at least once a month (of which most either organized or helped to run an event – usually a sporting event – or participated in raising money for one).
- The share of people informally volunteering at least once a month (for example, to help elderly neighbours) fell to 29 per cent, down from 35 per cent the previous year. The share giving

informal help at least once a year fell from 62 to
54 per cent.
– Charitable giving continued its decline since 2005.

What is happening? For Putnam, it is primarily
technology – first television, then the internet – that has
been the death of traditional associational life in America.
But I take a different view. Facebook and its ilk create social
networks that are huge but weak. With 900 million active
users – nine times the number in 2008 – Facebook's
network is a vast tool enabling like-minded people to
exchange like-minded opinions about, well, what they
like. Maybe, as Jared Cohen and Eric Schmidt argue,
the consequences of such exchanges will indeed be
revolutionary – though just how far Google or Facebook
really played a decisive role in the Arab Spring is debatable.[20]
(After all, Libyans did more than just unfriend Colonel
Gaddafi.) But I doubt very much that online communities
are a substitute for traditional forms of association.

Could I have cleared the beach by 'poking' my Facebook
friends or creating a new Facebook group? I doubt it. A
2007 study revealed that most users in fact treat Facebook as
a way to maintain contact with existing friends, often ones
they no longer see regularly because they no longer live near
by. The students surveyed were two and half times more
likely to use Facebook this way than to initiate connections
with strangers – which is what I had to do to clear the beach.[21]

It is not technology that has hollowed out civil society.

It is something Tocqueville himself anticipated, in what is perhaps the most powerful passage in *Democracy in America*. Here, he vividly imagines a future society in which associational life has died:

> I see an innumerable crowd of like and equal men who revolve on themselves without repose, procuring the small and vulgar pleasures with which they fill their souls. Each of them, withdrawn and apart, is like a stranger to the destiny of all the others: his children and his particular friends form the whole human species for him; as for dwelling with his fellow citizens, he is beside them, but he does not see them; he touches them and does not feel them; he exists only in himself and for himself alone . . .
>
> Above these an immense tutelary power is elevated, which alone takes charge of assuring their enjoyments and watching over their fate. It is absolute, detailed, regular, far-seeing, and mild. It would resemble paternal power if, like that, it had for its object to prepare men for manhood; but on the contrary, it seeks only to keep them fixed irrevocably in childhood . . .
>
> Thus, after taking each individual by turns in its powerful hands and kneading him as it likes, the sovereign extends its arms over society as a whole; it covers its surface with a network of small, complicated, painstaking, uniform rules through which the most original minds and the most vigorous souls cannot clear a way to surpass the crowd; it does not break wills, but it softens them, bends them, and directs

them; it rarely forces one to act, but it constantly opposes itself to one's acting; it does not destroy, it prevents things from being born; it does not tyrannize, it hinders, compromises, enervates, extinguishes, dazes, and finally reduces each nation to being nothing more than a herd of timid and industrious animals of which the government is the shepherd.[22]

Tocqueville was surely right. Not technology, but the state – with its seductive promise of 'security from the cradle to the grave' – was the real enemy of civil society. Even as he wrote, he recorded and condemned the first attempts to have 'a government . . . take the place of some of the greatest American associations'.

But what political power would ever be in a state to suffice for the innumerable multitude of small undertakings that American citizens execute every day with the aid of an association? . . . The more it puts itself in place of associations, the more particular persons, losing the idea of associating with each other, will need it to come to their aid . . .

The morality and intelligence of a democratic people would risk no fewer dangers than its business and its industry if the government came to take the place of associations everywhere.

Sentiments and ideas renew themselves, the heart is enlarged, and the human mind is developed only by the reciprocal action of men upon one another.[23]

Amen to that.

Privatizing Schools

To see just how right that wise old Frenchman was, ask yourself: how many clubs do you belong to? For my part, I count three London clubs, one in Oxford, one in New York and one in Cambridge, Massachusetts. I am a deplorably inactive member, but I pay my dues and use the sports facilities, the dining facilities and the guest rooms several times a year. I give regularly, though not enough, to two charities. I belong to one gymnasium. I support a soccer club.

I am probably most active as an alumnus of the principal educational institutions I attended in my youth: the Glasgow Academy and Magdalen College, Oxford. I also regularly give time to the schools my children attend, as well as to the university where I teach. Let me explain why I am so partial to these independent* educational institutions.

The view I am about to state is highly unfashionable. At a lunch held by the *Guardian* newspaper, I elicited gasps of horror when I uttered the following words: in my opinion, the best institutions in the British Isles today are the independent schools. (Needless to say, those who gasped loudest had all attended such schools.) If there is one educational

* Strictly speaking, Magdalen is part of a state-funded university, the independence of which has intermittently been challenged by the government. But the college remains a self-governing entity with its own endowment.

policy I would like to see adopted throughout the United Kingdom, it would be a policy that aimed to increase significantly the number of private educational institutions – and, at the same time, to establish programmes of vouchers, bursaries and scholarships to allow a substantial number of children from lower-income families to attend them.

Of course, this is the kind of thing that the left reflexively denounces as 'elitist'. Even some Conservatives, like George Walden, regard private schools as a cause of inequality, institutions so pernicious that they should be abolished. Let me explain why such views are utterly wrong.

For about a hundred years, no doubt, the expansion of public education was a good thing. As Peter Lindert has pointed out, schools were the exception that proved Tocqueville's rule, for it was the American states that led the way in setting up local taxes to fund universal and indeed compulsory schooling after 1852. With few exceptions, widening the franchise elsewhere in the world led swiftly to the adoption of similar systems. This was economically important, because the returns to universal education were high: literate and numerate people are much more productive workers.[24] But we need to recognize the limits of public monopolies in education, especially for societies that have long ago achieved mass literacy. The problem is that public monopoly providers of education suffer from the same problems that afflict monopoly providers of anything: quality declines because of lack of competition and the creeping power of vested 'producer' interests.

We also need to acknowledge, no matter what our ideological prejudices, that there is a good reason why private educational institutions play a crucial role in setting and raising educational standards all over the world.

I am not arguing for private schools against state schools. I am arguing for both, because 'biodiversity' is preferable to monopoly. A mix of public and private institutions with meaningful competition favours excellence. That is why American universities (which operate within an increasingly global competitive system) are the best in the world – twenty-two out of the world's top thirty according to rankings by Shanghai Jiao Tong University – while American high schools (in a localized monopoly system) are generally rather bad – witness the 2009 results of the Programme for International Student Assessment for mathematical attainment at age fifteen. Would Harvard be Harvard if it had at some point been nationalized by either the State of Massachusetts or the federal government? You know the answer.

In the United Kingdom, we have the opposite system: it is the universities that have essentially been reduced to agencies of a government-financed National Higher Education Service – despite the advent in England and Wales of top-up fees that are still below what the best institutions should be charging – whereas there is a lively and financially unconstrained independent sector in secondary education. The results? Apart from the elite, which retain their own resources and/or reputations, most UK universities are in a state of crisis. Only seven made it into *The Times Higher*

Education Supplement's latest global top fifty. Yet we boast some of the finest secondary schools on the planet.

The apologists of traditional state education need to grasp a simple point: by providing 'free' state schooling that is generally of mediocre quality, you incentivize the emergence of a really good private system (since nobody is going to pay between £10,000 and £30,000 a year for an education that is just a wee bit better than the free option).[25]

It is rather ironic that, at the time of writing, the policies being introduced to address the problem of low-quality public education in England are the responsibility of a Scotsman. Michael Gove picked up the idea from an Old Fettesian named Tony Blair: turning failing schools into self-governing academies. Between 2010 and 2012, the number of academies went from just 200 to approaching half of all secondary schools. Schools like Mossbourne Academy in Hackney or Durand Academy, a primary in Stockwell, show what can be achieved even in impoverished neighbourhoods when the dead hand of local authority control is removed.[26] Even more promising are the new 'free schools' being set up by parents, teachers and others, like Toby Young, who has finally worked out the real way to win friends and influence people.[27] Notice that these schools are not selective. They remain state funded. But their increased autonomy has swiftly led to much higher standards of both discipline and learning.

There are many on the left who deplore these developments. (Many Labour MPs would happily disown the very idea of academies.) Yet they are part of a global trend. All over the world, smart countries are moving away from the outdated model of state education monopolies and allowing civil society back into education, where it belongs.

Many people erroneously believe that Scandinavia is a place where the old-fashioned welfare state is alive and well. In fact, only Finland has maintained a strict state monopoly on education, the success of which makes that country the exception that proves my rule. By contrast, Sweden and Denmark have been pioneers of educational reform. Thanks to a bold scheme of decentralization and vouchers, the number of independent schools has soared in Sweden. Denmark's 'free' schools are independently run and receive a government grant per pupil, but are able to charge fees and raise funds in other ways if they can justify doing so in terms of results. (Similar reforms have meant that around two-thirds of Dutch students are now in independent schools.)[28]

Today in the United States, there are more than 2,000 charter schools – like English academies, publicly funded but independently run – bringing choice in education to around 2 million families in some of the country's poorest urban areas. Organizations like Success Academy have to endure vilification and intimidation from the US teachers' unions precisely because the higher standards at their charter schools pose such a threat to the status quo of under-performance and under-achievement. In New York City's public schools, 62 per cent of third, fourth and fifth graders passed their maths exams last year. The latest figure at Harlem Success Academy was 99 per cent. For science it was 100 per cent.[29] And this is not because the charter schools cherry-pick the best students or attract the most motivated parents. Students are admitted to Harlem Success by lottery. They do better because the school is both accountable and autonomous.

There is, however, a further step that still needs to be taken. That step is to increase the number of schools that are truly independent, in the sense of being privately funded; and truly free, in the sense of being free to select pupils. Significantly, six out of ten UK academy heads said in a March 2012 survey that the national agreement on pay and conditions prevents them from paying effective teachers more money, or extending the school day to give weaker pupils extra tuition.[30] There are no such inhibitions about private education elsewhere. In Sweden companies like Kunskapsskolan ('The Knowledge School') are educating tens of thousands of pupils. In Brazil, private school chains like Objetivo, COC and Pitágoras are teaching literally hundreds of thousands of students. Perhaps the most remarkable case, however, is India. There, as James Tooley has shown, the best hope of a decent education in the slums of cities like Hyderabad comes from private schools like the imaginatively named Royal Grammar School, Little Nightingale's High School or Firdaus Flowers Convent School.[31] Tooley and his researchers have found similar private schools in parts of Africa too. Invariably, they are a response to atrociously bad public schools, where class sizes are absurdly large and teachers are frequently asleep or absent.

The problem in Britain is not that there are too many private schools. The problem is that there are too few – and if their charitable status is ultimately revoked, there will be even fewer. Only around 7 per cent of British teenagers are in private schools, about the same proportion as in the United States. If you want to know one of the reasons why Asian teenagers do so much better than their British and American peers in standardized tests, it is this: private schools educate more than a quarter of pupils in Macao, Hong Kong, South Korea, Taiwan and Japan. The average PISA maths score for those places is 10 per cent higher than for the UK and the US. The gap between them and us is as large as the gap between us and Turkey. It is no coincidence that the share of Turkish students in private schools is below 4 per cent.

Private education benefits more people than just the elite. In a 2010 article, Martin West and Ludger Woessmann demonstrated that 'a 10 per cent increase in enrolment in private schools improves a country's mathematics test scores . . . by almost half a year's worth of learning. A 10 per cent increase in private school enrolment also reduces the total educational spending per student by over 5 per cent of the OECD average.'[32] In other words, more private education means higher-quality and more efficient education for everyone. A perfect illustration is the way Wellington College is now sponsoring a publicly funded academy. Another is the way schools like Rugby and Glasgow Academy are expanding their bursary schemes, aiming to increase the proportion of pupils whose fees are covered from the school's own resources.

The education revolution of the twentieth century was that basic education became available to most people in democracies. The education revolution of the twenty-first century will be that good education will become available to an increasing proportion of children. If you are against that, then you are the true elitist: you are the one who wants to keep poor kids in lousy schools.

A Bigger Society

The larger story I am telling, using education as the example, is that over the past fifty years governments encroached too far on the realm of civil society. That had its benefits where (as in the case of primary education) there was insufficient private provision. But there were real costs, too.

Like Tocqueville, I believe that spontaneous local activism by citizens is better than central state action not just in terms of its results, but more importantly in terms of its effect on us as citizens. For true citizenship is not just about voting, earning and staying on the right side of the law. It is also about participating in the 'troop' – the wider group beyond our families – which is precisely where we learn how to develop and enforce rules of conduct: in short, to govern ourselves. To educate our children. To care for the helpless. To fight crime. To keep the streets clean.

Since the phrase 'big society' entered the British political lexicon, abuse has been heaped upon it. In the same month that I delivered the lectures on which this book is based (June 2012), the Archbishop of Canterbury called it 'aspirational waffle designed to conceal a deeply damaging withdrawal of the state from its responsibilities to the most vulnerable'.[33] Even Martin Sime, the chief executive of the Scottish Council of Voluntary Organizations – who claims to believe in 'self-help' – has described the big society as a 'toxic brand . . . a Tory con trick and a cover for cuts'.[34] It will be clear by now that I am much more sympathetic than these gentlemen to the idea that our society – and indeed most societies – would benefit from more private initiative and less dependence on the state. If that is now a conservative position, so be it. Once, it was considered the essence of true liberalism.

In the preceding pages, I have tried to argue that we are living through a profound crisis of the institutions that were the keys to our previous success – not only economic, but also political and cultural – as a civilization. I have represented the crisis of public debt, the single biggest problem facing Western politics, as a symptom of the betrayal of future generations: a breach of Edmund Burke's social contract between the present and the future.

I have suggested that the attempt to use complex regulation to avert future financial crises is based on a profound misunderstanding of the way the market economy works: a misunderstanding into which Walter Bagehot never fell.

I have warned that the rule of law, so crucial to the operation of both democracy and capitalism, is in danger of degenerating into the rule of lawyers: a danger Charles Dickens well knew.

And, finally, I have proposed that our once vibrant civil society is in a state of decay, not so much because of technology, but because of the excessive pretensions of the state: a threat that Tocqueville presciently warned Europeans and Americans against.

We humans live in a complex matrix of institutions. There is government. There is the market. There is the law. And then there is civil society. Once – I'm tempted to date it from the time of the Scottish Enlightenment – this matrix worked astonishingly well, with each set of institutions complementing and reinforcing the rest. That, I believe, was the key to Western success in the eighteenth, nineteenth and twentieth centuries. But the institutions in our times are out of joint.

It is our challenge, in the years that lie ahead, to restore them – to reverse the Great Degeneration – and to return to those first principles of a truly free society which I have tried to affirm, with a little help from some of the great thinkers of the past.

It is time, in short, to clear up the beach.

Conclusion

Inequalities Explained

Why are some countries so much richer than others? To be precise, why are real wages – wages adjusted for the cost of living – higher in some countries than in others? Real wages in London were more than seven times higher than in Canton on the eve of the First World War, whereas they had been roughly comparable (allowing for differences in patterns of consumption) 200 years before.[1] This was despite the fact that between 1700 and 1900 the world economy became far more integrated, with unprecedented flows of capital, goods and labour. Today, in another age of globalization, we encounter similar differentials. Manufacturing wages in China are no longer one-twentieth of the US level, as they were in 2005; indeed, they are projected to rise from one-tenth to one-fifth of American wages between 2012 and 2015. In purchasing-power parity terms, the gap is already even narrower. The number of Big Macs an employee of McDonald's can buy with an hour of work is just four times higher in the United States than in China.[2] Yet that is still a significant gap.

While there is a consensus that such differentials are related to differences in 'total factor productivity', there is little agreement as to what is responsible for such differences. Explanations that emphasize the role of geography, climate, disease or natural-resource endowments are less convincing today than they seemed in the eighteenth century. Scientific knowledge, technological innovation and market integration have greatly reduced the significance of distance, weather and germs, while mineral wealth has been revealed to be as much a curse as a blessing. Explanations that assert racial differences in intelligence or industriousness are no longer taken seriously. There are pronounced differences in IQ between genetically indistinguishable populations, such as West and East Germans before 1991, or the Irish and Irish-Americans in around 1970. We can also trace far more rapid changes in average IQ over time than can be explained in terms of biology.[3] The roles of religion, culture or 'national character' have also long intrigued sociologists. But the evidence of economic history is that shifts from poverty to prosperity generally happen too suddenly and in too many different cultural milieus to be explained in such terms.

In any case, the differences in economic welfare within countries are in some ways just as big as the differences between them. In 2007 the average income of Americans in the top 1 per cent in terms of income was thirty times that of the average income of Americans in the remaining 99 per cent. This is another differential that has changed rapidly in recent years – but, unlike inter-country inequality, intra-country inequality has been increasing rather than diminishing. In 1978 the top percentile was just ten times richer than everyone else. By most measures, American society is as unequal today as it was in the late 1920s.[4] Another way of putting this is that a massive proportion of the benefits of the last thirty-five years of economic growth has gone to the super-elite. That was not true in the period between the Great Depression of the 1930s and the Great Inflation of the 1970s. Between 1933 and 1973 the average real income of the 99 per cent rose (before tax) by a factor of four and a half. Yet from 1973 until 2010 it actually fell.[5]

So what exactly is going on? As we have seen, narrowly economic explanations that focus on the impact of financial forces ('deleveraging'), international integration ('globalization'), the role of information technology ('off-shoring' and 'outsourcing') or fiscal policy ('stimulus' versus 'austerity') do not offer sufficient explanations. We need to delve into the history of institutions to understand the complex dynamics of convergence and divergence that characterize today's world. The democratic deficits of Chapter 1, the regulatory fragility of Chapter 2, the rule of lawyers of Chapter 3 and the uncivil society of Chapter 4:

these offer better explanations of why the West is now delivering lower growth and greater inequality than in the past – in other words, why it is now the West that finds itself in Adam Smith's stationary state.

The Urban Future

In these concluding pages, I want to ask what my diagnosis of a great institutional degeneration in the Western world implies about the future. To answer that question it is helpful to borrow former US Defense Secretary Donald Rumsfeld's famous typology of 'known knowns', 'known unknowns' and 'unknown unknowns' – but to add a fourth category: 'unknown knowns'. These are the future scenarios that are quite well known to students of history, but which are ignored by everybody else.

Let us begin with the known knowns. Aside from the laws of physics and chemistry, the following things are unlikely to change significantly in the foreseeable future: the normal (or bell-curve) distribution of intelligence in any population, the cognitive biases of the human mind, and our evolved biological behaviours. We can also assume that the global population will continue to rise towards nine billion, though with nearly all of the increase concentrated in Africa and South Asia, and that in the rest of the world the age structure will tilt further in the direction of the elderly. On the other hand, at least some key commodities – base metals and rare earths in particular – will remain in finite supply. However, the pace of global technological diffusion seems likely to remain high and this will encourage the continued migration of people from the country to the cities. The developing world's new 'megacities' – conurbations with populations of more than ten million – will thus play a defining role in the twenty-first century. There are already twenty of these: six (led by Shanghai) in China, three (led by Mumbai) in India, along with Mexico City, São Paolo, Dhaka, Karachi, Buenos Aires, Manila, Rio de Janeiro, Moscow, Cairo, Istanbul and Lagos. They, along with 420 other non-Western cities, could generate close to half of all the growth between 2012 and 2025, according the McKinsey Global Institute.[6]

In many ways, this is an exciting prospect. The physicist Geoffrey West has shown that there are both economies of scale (in infrastructure) and increasing returns to scale (in human creativity) from the process of urbanization. In his words: 'Cities are . . . the cause of the good life. They are the centres of wealth creation, creativity, innovation, and invention. They're the exciting places. They are these magnets that suck people in.' West and his colleagues at the Santa Fe Institute have identified two remarkable statistical regularities. First, 'every infrastructural quantity . . . from total length of roadways to the length of electrical lines to the length of gas lines . . . scaled in the same way as the number of gas stations.' That is to say, the bigger the city, the fewer gas stations were needed per capita, an economy of scale with a fairly consistent exponent of around 0.85 (meaning that, when a city's population increases by 100 per cent, it needs to increase the number of gas stations per capita by only 85 per cent). Secondly, and more surprisingly:

> Socioeconomic . . . things like wages, the number of educational institutions, the number of patents produced, et cetera . . . scaled in what we called a super-linear fashion. Instead of being an exponent less than one, indicating economies of scale, the exponent was bigger than one, indicating . . . increasing returns to scale . . . That says that systematically, the bigger the city, the more wages you can expect, the more educational institutions in principle, [the] more cultural events, [the] more patents are produced, it's more innovative and so on. Remarkably, all to the same degree. There was a universal exponent which turned out to be approximately 1.15, which . . . says something like the following: If you double the size of a city from 50,000 to a hundred thousand, a million to two million, five million to ten million . . . systematically, you get a roughly 15 per cent increase in productivity, patents, the number of research institutions, wages [per capita] . . . and you get systematically a 15 per cent saving in length of roads and general infrastructure.[7]

People even walk disproportionately faster in big cities than in small ones. There is a disproportionately wider range of possible jobs to do. All this is best explained in terms of network effects. True, there are equally large negative externalities: bigger cities have disproportionately bigger problems with crime, disease and pollution. But provided we can innovate fast enough, West argues, our megacities can avoid – or at least postpone – the moment of collapse.*

West's analysis explains why the process of urbanization – which is in many ways at the heart of the history of civilization – is more than exponential. Although his data are drawn from all over the world, however, we know that there is a major difference in the benefits of urbanization between New York or London, on the one hand, and Mumbai or Lagos, on the other. In late July 2012, a massive failure of the power grid in northern India – which deprived 640 million people of electricity – provided a reminder that megacities are very fragile networks. We know, too, that at times in New York's history – notably the late 1980s, when violent crime peaked – the negative externalities of urban networks came close to outweighing the positives.

The argument of this book implies that the net benefits

---

* In West's words: 'One of the bad things about open-ended growth, growing faster than exponentially, is that open-ended growth eventually leads to collapse. It leads to collapse mathematically because of something called finite times singularity. You hit something that's called a singularity, which is a technical term, and it turns out as you approach this singularity, the system, if it reaches it, will collapse.'

of urbanization are conditioned by the institutional framework within which cities operate. Where there is effective representative government, where there is a dynamic market economy, where the rule of law is upheld and where civil society is independent from the state, the benefits of a dense population overwhelm the costs. Where these conditions do not pertain, the opposite applies. Put differently, in a secure institutional framework, urban networks are what Nassim Taleb calls 'anti-fragile': they evolve in ways that are not only resilient in the face of perturbations, but actually gain strength from them (like London during the Blitz). But where that framework is lacking, urban networks are fragile: they can collapse in the face of a relatively small shock (like Rome when attacked by the Visigoths in AD 410).

Shooters and Diggers

In the Spaghetti Western *The Good, the Bad and the Ugly*, there is a memorable scene that sums up the world economy today. Blondie (Clint Eastwood) and Tuco (Eli Wallach) have finally found the cemetery where they know the gold they seek is buried – a vast Civil War graveyard. Eastwood looks at his gun, looks at Wallach and utters the immortal line: 'In this world, there are two kinds of people, my friend. Those with loaded guns . . . and those who dig.'

In the post-crisis economic order, there are likewise two kinds of economies. Those with vast accumulations of assets, including sovereign wealth funds (currently in excess of $4 trillion) and hard-currency reserves ($5.5 trillion for emerging markets alone), are the ones with loaded guns. The economies with huge public debts (which now total nearly $50 trillion worldwide), by contrast, are the ones that have to dig. In such a world, it pays to have underground resources. But these are not distributed at all fairly. By my calculations, the estimated market value of the world's proven subsoil mineral reserves is around $359 trillion, of which over 60 per cent is owned by just ten countries: Russia, the United States, Australia, Saudi Arabia, China, Guinea (which is rich in bauxite), Iran, Venezuela, South Africa and Kazakhstan.[8]

Now we enter the realm of the known unknowns. We do not know by how much resource discoveries (especially in unsurveyed Africa) and technological advances (such as hydraulic fracturing) will increase the supply of natural resources in the years to come. Nor do we know what impact financial crises will have on commodity prices and therefore the incentive to exploit new sources of fuel and material. Finally, we do not know with any certainty how politics will affect a sector that is more vulnerable to expropriation and arbitrary taxation than any other because of the immobile nature of its assets. We know that the unrestricted burning of fossil fuels is likely to lead to changes in the earth's climate, but we do not know exactly what these will be or when they will be disruptive enough to generate a meaningful policy response. Until then, the West will indulge itself with fantasies about 'green' energy, and the Rest will continue to burn coal as fast as it can be dug up, instead of doing the things that would really reduce carbon dioxide emissions: building nuclear and clean-coal power-plants, converting vehicles to natural gas and increasing the energy efficiency of the average home.[9] All these known unknowns explain the extraordinary whipsaw movements in commodity prices that we have witnessed since 2002.

Also in the category of known unknowns belong two distinct kinds of natural disaster: earthquakes and the associated tsunamis they cause, which are randomly generated by the movements of the earth's tectonic plates (so we know their location but not their timing or magnitude), and pandemics, which arise from the similarly random mutation of viruses like influenza. The most that can be said about these two threats to humanity is that they will kill many more people in the future than in the past because of the increasing concentration of our species in cities in the Asia-Pacific region which, perversely, are often located close to fault lines because of the human fondness for coastal locations. Add to this the problem of nuclear proliferation, and it does not seem unreasonable to regard the world as a more dangerous place than it was during the Cold War, when the principal threat to mankind was the calculable risk of a worst-case outcome to a simple two-player game. Today we face more uncertainty than calculable risk. Such is the result of exchanging a bipolar world for a networked one.

By their very nature, the unknown unknowns are impossible to anticipate. But what of the unknown knowns – the insights that history has to offer, which most people choose to ignore? Asked in late 2011 to name 'the key risks that could derail growth in fast-growth markets over the next three years', nearly a thousand global business executives identified asset-price bubbles, political corruption, inequality of income and failure to tackle inflation as the four biggest.[10] By 2014, these fears may seem misplaced. From an historian's point of view, the real risks in the non-Western world today are of revolution and war. These are precisely the events we should expect under the circumstances described above. Revolutions are caused by a combination of food-price spikes, a youthful population, a rising middle class, a disruptive ideology, a corrupt old regime and a weakening international order. All these conditions are present in the Middle East today – and of course the Islamist revolution is already well under way, albeit under the misleading Western label of the 'Arab Spring'. The thing to worry about is the war that nearly always follows a revolution of such magnitude. For despite Steven Pinker's optimistic claim that the long-run trend of human history is away from violence, the statistical incidence of war exhibits no such pattern.[11] Like earthquakes, we know where wars are likely to occur, but we cannot know when they will break out or how big they will be.

Against 'Technoptimism'

Revolution and war are not new threats. In the eighteenth century the disruptive ideology that grew out of the Enlightenment became the basis for two major challenges to the Anglophone empire that then bestrode the globe. In fighting revolution on both sides of the Atlantic, the British state accumulated a very large public debt, mainly as a result of its wars against revolutionary France. By the end of the Napoleonic era, the national debt exceeded 250 per cent of GDP. Yet the subsequent deleveraging – which reduced the debt burden by an order of magnitude to just 25 per cent of GDP – was perhaps the most successful in recorded history. Inflation played no role whatsoever. The British government consistently ran peacetime primary surpluses, thanks to a combination of fiscal discipline and a growth rate higher than the rate of interest. This 'beautiful deleveraging'* was not without its ugly episodes, notably in the mid-1820s and late 1840s, when austerity policies caused social unrest (and failed to alleviate a disastrous famine in Ireland). Nevertheless, the deleveraging process coincided with the key phase of the first Industrial Revolution – the

---

* The phrase was coined by the American hedge-fund manager Ray Dalio, whose hedge fund Bridgewater performed exceptionally well during the financial crisis.

railway mania – and the expansion of the British Empire to very nearly its maximum extent. The lesson of history is that a country that achieves technological innovation and profitable geopolitical expansion can grow its way out from under a mountain of debt.[12]

Can the United States emulate this feat? I doubt it. First, the evidence suggests that it is very hard to achieve higher growth under a heavy debt burden. In their study of twenty-six episodes of 'debt overhang' – cases when public debt in advanced countries exceeded 90 per cent of GDP for at least five years – Carmen and Vincent Reinhart and Ken Rogoff show that debt overhangs were associated with lower growth (of 1.2 percentage points of GDP) over protracted periods (lasting an average of twenty-three years), lowering the level of output by nearly a quarter relative to the pre-overhang trend.[13] Significantly, the negative impact on growth was not necessarily the result of higher real interest rates. A crucial point is the non-linear character of the relationship between debt and growth. Because the debt burden lowers growth only when it rises above the 90 per cent of GDP threshold, the habit of running deficits gets well established before it becomes deleterious. This evidence poses a serious problem for those Keynesian economists who believe that the correct response to a reduction in aggregate demand via private sector deleveraging is for the already indebted public sector to borrow even more. It also casts doubt on the validity of the claim that low interest rates on US Treasuries are a market signal that the government can and should issue more debt.[14]

Equally remote is the prospect that a technological break-through comparable with the railways could provide the United States with a 'get out of jail' card. The harsh reality is that, from the vantage point of 2012, the next twenty-five years (2013–38) are highly unlikely to see more dramatic changes than science and technology produced in the last twenty-five (1987–2012). For a start, the end of the Cold War and the Asian economic miracle provided one-off, non-repeatable stimuli to the process of innovation in the form of a massive reduction in labour costs and therefore the price of hardware not to mention all those ex-Soviet PhDs who could finally do something useful. The IT revolution that began in the 1980s was important in terms of its productivity impact inside the US – though even this should not be exaggerated – but we are surely now in the realm of diminishing returns (the symptoms of which are deflation plus underemployment due partly to automation of unskilled work). Likewise, the breakthroughs in medical science we can expect as a result of the successful map-ping of the human genome will probably result in further extensions of the average lifespan, but if we make no commensurate advances in neuroscience – if we succeed in protracting the life of the body but not of the mind – the net economic consequences will be negative, because we will simply increase the number of dependent elderly.

My pessimism about the likelihood of a technological

deus ex machina is supported by a simple historical observation. The achievements of the last twenty-five years were not especially impressive compared with what we did in the preceding twenty-five years, 1961–86 (for example, landing men on the moon). And the technological milestones of the twenty-five years before that, 1935–60, were even more remarkable (such as splitting the atom). In the words of Peter Thiel, perhaps the lone sceptic within a hundred miles of Palo Alto, 'We wanted flying cars, instead we got 140 characters.'* Travel speeds have declined since the days of Concorde. Green energy is 'unaffordable energy'. And we lack the ambition to 'declare war' on Alzheimer's disease, 'even though nearly a third of America's 85-year-olds suffer from some form of dementia'.[15] Moreover, technological optimists have to explain why the rapid scientific technological progress in those earlier periods coincided with massive conflict between armed ideologies. (Question: Which was the world's most scientifically advanced society in 1932, in terms of Nobel Prize-winners in the sciences? Answer: Germany.) The implications are clear. More and faster information is not good in itself. Knowledge is not always the cure. And network effects are not always positive. There was great technological progress during the 1930s. But it did not end the Depression. That took a world war.

Weary of counter-insurgency warfare and wakening up

---

* The maximum length of a Twitter 'tweet'.

to the fossil-fuel riches made accessible by 'fracking' – which could end its reliance on Middle Eastern oil by 2035 – the United States is rapidly winding up four decades of hegemony in that region. No one knows who or what will fill the vacuum. A nuclear Iran? A neo-Ottoman Turkey? Arab Islamists led by the Muslim Brotherhood? Whoever emerges on top, they are unlikely to get there without bloodshed. Ask anyone who works in the shadowy world of intelligence to list the biggest threats we face, and they will probably include bio-terrorism, cyber war and nuclear proliferation. What these things have in common, of course, is the way modern technology can empower radicalized (or just plain crazy) individuals and groups. It will surely not be long before another unknown known becomes apparent to non-historians: that it is when empires retreat, not when they advance, that violence reaches its peak. And the violence can manifest itself in the imperial heartland too. The 'cliometrician' Peter Turchin argues that 'the next instability peak [of violence] should occur in the United States around 2020'.[16]

You Didn't Build That

Countries arrive at the stationary state, as Adam Smith argued, when their 'laws and institutions' degenerate to the point that elite rent-seeking dominates the economic and political process. I have tried to suggest that this is the case in important parts of the Western world today. Public debt – stated and implicit – has become a way for the older generation to live at the expense of the young and the unborn. Regulation has become dysfunctional to the point of increasing the fragility of the system. Lawyers, who can be revolutionaries in a dynamic society, become parasites in a stationary one. And civil society withers into a mere no man's land between corporate interests and big government. Taken together, these are the things I refer to as the Great Degeneration.

On July 13, 2012, as I was completing this book, the President of the United States gave a speech that neatly illustrated the point:

> If you were successful, somebody along the line gave you some help. There was a great teacher somewhere in your life. Somebody helped to create this unbelievable American system that we have that allowed you to thrive. Somebody invested in roads and bridges. If you've got a business – you didn't build that. Somebody else made that happen. The Internet didn't get invented on its own. Government research created the Internet so that all the companies could make money off the Internet.
>
> . . . There are some things, just like fighting fires, we don't do on our own . . . So we say to ourselves, ever since the founding of this country, you know what, there are

some things we do better together. That's how we funded the GI Bill. That's how we created the middle class. That's how we built the Golden Gate Bridge or the Hoover Dam. That's how we invented the Internet. That's how we sent a man to the moon.[17]

This surely is the authentic voice of the stationary state: the chief mandarin, addressing distant subjects in the provinces. It is not that the implied interdependence of the private sector and the state is wrong. It is the over-statement of the case that is disquieting, as if it took government to build every small business or, indeed, to 'create the middle class'. Also striking is the conspicuous absence from the speech of any future project comparable with those cited from the past (the Manhattan Project would have been an even better example, but presumably it is not politically correct).

In the same way, President Obama's second inaugural address suggested that the appropriate yardstick for an effective government was 'whether it helps families find jobs at a decent wage, care they can afford, a retirement that is dignified'. By contrast, 'without a watchful eye, the market can spin out of control'. The words 'debt' and 'deficit' were not mentioned. The dangers of excessive regulation and litigation were ignored. And civil society scarcely featured at all, as if the hallowed phrase 'we the people' is now synonymous with 'the government'.

It is bad enough to see state capitalism touted as an economic model by the Chinese Communist Party. But to hear it deployed by the President of the United States as a rhetorical trope nearly devoid of practical content makes this writer, for one, pine for the glad, confident morning of 1989 – when it really seemed the West had won, and a great regeneration had begun.

Notes

Introduction

1. Francis Fukuyama, 'The End of History and the Last Man', *National Interest*, 16 (Summer 1989), pp. 3–18.
2. McKinsey Global Institute, *Urban World: Cities and the Rise of the Consuming Class* (June 2012).
3. McKinsey Global Institute, *Debt and Deleveraging: The Global Credit Bubble and its Economic Consequences* (January 2010).
4. Peter Berezin, 'The Weak U. S. Labor Market: Mainly a Cyclical Problem . . . for Now', *Bank Credit Analyst*, 64, 1 (July 2012), p. 40.
5. See e.g. Jeffrey Sachs, *The Price of Civilization: Reawakening American Virtue and Prosperity* (New York, 2011).
6. See e.g. International Monetary Fund, 'Navigating the Fiscal Challenges Ahead', *Fiscal Monitor*, 14 May 2010.
7. Anthony B. Atkinson, Thomas Piketty and Emmanuel Saez, 'Top Incomes in the Long Run of History', *Journal of Economic Literature*, 49, 1 (2011), pp. 3–71.
8. Credit Suisse, *Global Wealth Databook* (October 2010), tables 3-1, 3-3 and 3-4.

9. For a brilliant analysis, see Jamil Baz, 'Current Crisis Merely a Warm-up Act', *Financial Times*, 11 July 2012.

10. Niall Ferguson, 'Too Big to Live: Why We Must Stamp Out State Monopoly Capitalism', *Adam Smith Review*, 6 (2011), pp. 327–40.

11. Juan Enriquez, 'Medicine's Missing Measure', *Atlantic* (May 2012): http://www.theatlantic.com/health/archive/2012/05/medicines-missing-measure/257901/.

12. John Stossel, 'I Tried to Open a Lemonade Stand', *Townhall*, 24 February 2012.

13. Tom Hertz, 'Rags, Riches, and Race: Intergenerational Income Mobility of Black and White Families in the United States', in Samuel Bowles, Herbert Gintis and Melissa Osborne (eds.), *Unequal Chances: Family Background and Economic Success* (New York, 2005), table 10.

14. Charles Murray, *Coming Apart: The State of White America, 1960–2010* (New York, 2012).

15. Adam Smith, *The Wealth of Nations* (1776), book I, ch. 8.

16. Ibid., ch. 9.

17. http://blog.lgiu.org.uk/2011/09/on-libya-and-institutions/. I am grateful to Lord Malloch-Brown for bringing these graffiti to my attention on BBC Radio 4's *Today* programme.

18. See most recently Daron Acemoglu and James A. Robinson, *Why Nations Fail: The Origins of Power, Prosperity, and Poverty* (New York, 2012). For a full discussion, see Chapter 1.

Chapter 1: The Human Hive

1. Richard Taverner, *The Garden of Wysdome Conteynynge Pleasaunt Floures, that is to say, Propre and Quycke Sayinges of Princes, Philosophers and other Sortes of Me[n]. Drawe[n] Forth of Good Aucthours* (London, 1539), p. 6.

2. Data from Angus Maddison, 'Statistics on World Population, GDP and Per Capita GDP, 1–2008 AD': http://www.ggdc.net/MADDISON/Historical_Statistics/vertical-file_02-2010.xls.

3. Data from World Bank, World Development Indicators online: http://data.worldbank.org/data-catalog/world-development-indicators.

4. Jared Diamond, *Guns, Germs and Steel: A Short History of Everybody for the Last 13,000 Years* (London, 1998). See also Ian Morris, *Why the West Rules – For Now: The Patterns of History, and What They Reveal About the Future* (New York, 2010).

5. Kenneth Pomeranz, *The Great Divergence: China, Europe and the Making of the Modern World Economy* (Princeton, 2000).

6. Douglass C. North, John Joseph Wallis and Barry R. Weingast, *Violence and Social Orders: A Conceptual Framework for Interpreting Recorded Human History* (Cambridge, 2009).

7. Francis Fukuyama, *The Origins of Political Order: From Prehuman Times to the French Revolution* (New York, 2011).

8. Daron Acemoglu and James A. Robinson, *Why Nations Fail: The Origins of Power, Prosperity, and Poverty* (New York, 2012), p. 4.

9. Ibid., pp. 7–9.

10. Paul Collier, *The Bottom Billion* (Oxford, 2007), pp. 50, 56; idem, *The Plundered Planet: How to Reconcile Prosperity with Nature* (London, 2010), pp. 47f., 58.

11. Hernando de Soto, *The Mystery of Capital: Why Capitalism Triumphs in the West and Fails Everywhere Else* (New York, 2000).

12. Hernando de Soto, 'The Free Market Secret of the Arab Revolutions', *Financial Times*, 8 November 2011.

13. J. C. D. Clark, 'British America: What If There Had Been No American Revolution?', in Niall Ferguson (ed.), *Virtual History: Alternatives and Counterfactuals* (London, 1993), pp. 125–75.

14. See e.g. J. R. Jones, 'The Revolution in Context', in idem (ed.), *Liberty Secured? Britain before and after 1688* (Stanford, 1992), p. 12.

15. Stephen C. A. Pincus and James A. Robinson, 'What Really Happened during the Glorious Revolution?', National Bureau of Economic Research Working Paper 17206 (July 2011).

16. Avner Greif, 'Institutions and the Path to the Modern Economy: Lessons from Medieval Trade', in C. Ménard and M. Shirley (eds.), *Handbook of New Institutional Economics* (Dordrecht, 2005), pp. 727–86.

17. Timur Kuran, *The Long Divergence: How Islamic Law Held Back the Middle East* (Princeton, 2010).

18. OECD, *PISA 2009 Results: What Students Know and Can Do: Student Performance in Reading, Mathematics and Science*

(Paris, 2010), p. 15: http://www.oecd.org/dataoecd/10/61/48852548.pdf.

19. Niall Ferguson, *Civilization: The West and the Rest* (London/New York, 2011).

20. Robert C. Allen, *The British Industrial Revolution in Global Perspective* (Cambridge, 2009).

21. Douglass C. North and Barry R. Weingast, 'Constitutions and Commitment: The Evolution of Institutions Governing Public Choice in Seventeenth-Century England', *Journal of Economic History*, 44, 4 (1989), pp. 803–32.

22. Laurence J. Kotlikoff and Scott Burns, *The Clash of Generations: Saving Ourselves, our Kids, and our Economy* (Cambridge, MA, 2012), p. 33.

23. Ibid., pp. 30f.

24. Roberto Cardarelli, James Sefton and Laurence J. Kotlikoff, 'Generational Accounting in the UK', *Economic Journal*, 110, 467, Features (November 2000), pp. F547–F574.

25. Carmen M. Reinhart and Kenneth S. Rogoff, 'Growth in a Time of Debt', NBER Working Paper 15639 (January 2010).

Chapter 2: The Darwinian Economy

1. See e.g. Paul Krugman, 'Reagan Did It', *New York Times*, 31 May 2009.

2. Idem, 'Financial Reform 101', *New York Times*, 1 April 2010. See also 'Punks and Plutocrats', *New York Times*, 28 March 2010.

3. Idem, 'Making Banking Boring', *New York Times*, 9 April 2009.

4. Idem, 'Egos and Immorality', *New York Times*, 24 May 2012. See also idem, 'Dimon's Déjà Vu Debacle', *New York Times*, 20 May 2012.

5. Simon Johnson and James Kwak, *Thirteen Bankers: The Wall Street Takeover and the Next Financial Meltdown* (New York, 2010).

6. Richard A. Posner, *The Crisis of Capitalist Democracy* (Cambridge, MA, 2010).

7. 'Wall Street Legend Sandy Weill: Break Up the Big Banks', CNBC.com, 25 July 2012.

8. David Kynaston, *The City of London*, vol. IV: *A Club No More, 1945–2000* (London, 2001).

9. Forest Capie, *The Bank of England: 1950s to 1979* (Cambridge, 2010), pp. 589ff.

10. See N. H. Dimsdale, 'British Monetary Policy since 1945', in N. F. R. Crafts and N. W. C. Woodward (eds.), *The British Economy since 1945* (Oxford, 1991), p. 108.

11. Niall Ferguson, 'Regulation and Deregulation in a Time of Stagflation: Siegmund Warburg and the City of London in the 1970s', paper presented at the European Association for Banking History, Brussels, 2010.

12. See e.g. Lord Turner, 'After the Crises: Assessing the Costs and Benefits of Financial Liberalisation', Fourteenth C. D. Deshmukh Memorial Lecture, Mumbai, 15 February 2010.

13. Idem, 'Debt and Deleveraging: Long Term and Short Term Challenges', Centre for Financial Studies, 21 November 2011.

14. Hugh Rockoff, 'Upon Daedalian Wings of Paper Money: Adam Smith and the Crisis of 1772', NBER Working Paper 15594 (December 2009).

15. Jessica Pressler, 'Look Who's Back', *New York Magazine*, 8 April 2012: http://nymag.com/news/business/themoney/john-mack-2012-4/index1.html.

16. Peter Wallison, 'Dodd–Frank's Liquidation Plan is Worse than Bankruptcy', *Bloomberg*, 11 June 2012.

17. Brooke Masters, 'Big Banks Need Extra $566bn, says Fitch', *Financial Times*, 17 May 2012.

18. Frances Darwin (ed.), *The Life and Letters of Charles Darwin, including an Autobiographical Chapter*, vol. I (London, 1887), p. 83.

19. Walter Bagehot, *Lombard Street: A Description of the Money Market* (London, 1896 [1873]), p. 11.

20. Niall Ferguson, 'An Evolutionary Approach to Financial History', *Cold Spring Harbor Symposia on Quantitative Biology*, 74 (2010), pp. 449–54.

21. Robert F. Weber, 'Structural Regulation as Antidote to Complexity Capture', *American Business Law Journal*, 49, 3 (2012).

22. For an accessible introduction, see Mark Buchanan, *Ubiquity: The Science of History . . . Or Why the World is Simpler Than We Think* (London, 2005).

23. Andrew Haldane, 'On Tackling the Credit Cycle and Too Big to Fail' (January 2011): http://www.iiea.com/event/

download_powerpoint?urlKey=andrew-haldane-on-fixing-finance. See also Henry Hu, 'Too Complex to Depict? Innovation, "Pure Information" and the SEC Disclosure Paradigm', *Texas Law Review* (June 2012).

24. Nassim Taleb, *Antifragile: Things that Gain from Disorder* (forthcoming).

25. Janos Kornai, *The Socialist System: The Political Economy of Communism* (Oxford, 1992).

26. Bagehot, *Lombard Street*, pp. 17, 160f.

27. Ibid., p. 165.

28. Ibid., pp. 58f.

29. Ibid., p. 199.

30. Ibid., p. 235.

31. Ibid., p. 325.

32. Ibid., p. 321.

33. Laurence J. Kotlikoff and John C. Goodman, 'Solving our Nation's Financial Crisis with Limited Purpose Banking', Boston University Working Paper (15 April 2009). See also John Kay, 'Narrow Banking: The Reform of Banking Regulation', Centre for the Study of Financial Innovation (2009).

34. Niall Ferguson, 'Too Big to Live: Why We Must Stamp Out State Monopoly Capitalism', *Adam Smith Review*, 6 (2011), pp. 327–40.

35. Bagehot, *Lombard Street*, p. 334.

36. Ibid., p. 336.

37. Gretchen Morgenson, 'Lending Magnate Settles Fraud Case', *New York Times*, 15 October 2010.

Chapter 3: The Landscape of Law

1. Chen Guangcheng, 'How China Flouts its Laws', *New York Times*, 29 May 2012.

2. He Weifang, 'China's First Steps towards Constitutionalism', in idem, *In the Name of Justice: Striving for the Rule of Law in China*.

3. Tom Bingham, *The Rule of Law* (London, 2010).

4. Ben Wilson, *What Price Liberty? How Freedom was Won and is Being Lost* (London, 2009).

5. Ronald Dworkin, *Law's Empire* (London, 1986), pp. 166, 225.

6. Ibid., p. 346.

7. Ronald Dworkin, *Justice for Hedgehogs* (Cambridge, MA, 2011), p. 402.

8. Douglass C. North, *Institutions, Institutional Change and Economic Performance* (Cambridge, 1990), p. 54.

9. Ibid., p. 59.

10. Avner Greif, 'Institutions and the Path to the Modern Economy: Lessons from Medieval Trade', in C. Ménard and M. Shirley (eds.), *Handbook of New Institutional Economics* (Dordrecht, 2005) , pp. 727–86.

11. Rafael La Porta, Florencio Lopez-de-Silanes, Andrei Shleifer and Robert W. Vichny, 'Legal Determinants of External Finance', *Journal of Finance*, 52, 3 (July 1997), pp. 1131–50.

12. Ibid.

13. Rafael La Porta, Florencio Lopez-de-Silanes, Andrei Shleifer and Robert Vishny, 'Investor Protection and

Corporate Governance', *Journal of Financial Economics*, 58 (2000), pp. 3–27.

14. Simeon Djankov, Rafael La Porta, Florencio Lopez-de-Silanes and Andrei Shleifer, 'The Regulation of Entry', *Quarterly Journal of Economics*, 117, 1 (February 2002), pp. 1–37.

15. Simeon Djankov, Rafael La Porta, Florencio Lopez-de-Silanes and Andrei Shleifer, 'Courts', *Quarterly Journal of Economics*, 118, 2 (May 2003), pp. 453–517.

16. Juan C. Botero, Simeon Djankov, Rafael La Porta, Florencio Lopez-de-Silanes and Andrei Shleifer, 'The Regulation of Labor', *Quarterly Journal of Economics*, 119, 4 (November 2004), pp. 1339–82.

17. Rafael La Porta, Florencio Lopez-de-Silanes and Andrei Shleifer, 'What Works in Securities Laws?', *Journal of Finance*, 61, 1 (February 2006), pp. 1–32.

18. Simeon Djankov, Oliver Hart, Caralee McLiesh and Andrei Shleifer, 'Debt Enforcement around the World', *Journal of Political Economy*, 116, 6 (2008), pp. 1105–49.

19. Rafael La Porta, Florencio Lopez-de-Silanes and Andrei Shleifer, 'The Economic Consequences of Legal Origins', *Journal of Economic Literature*, 46, 2 (June 2008), pp. 285–332.

20. Ibid., p. 300.

21. He Weifang, 'The Ongoing Quest for Judicial Independence in China (2001)', in idem, *In the Name of Justice*.

22. Greif, 'Institutions and the Path to the Modern Economy', pp. 766–8.

23. See e.g. Naomi R. Lamoreaux and Jean-Laurent Rosenthal, 'Legal Regime and Business's Organizational Choice: A Comparison of France and the United States during the Mid-Nineteenth Century', NBER Working Paper 10288 (February 2004); Naomi R. Lamoreaux and Jean-Laurent Rosenthal, 'Contractual Tradeoffs and SMEs' Choice of Organizational Form: A View from U.S. and French History, 1830–2000', NBER Working Paper 12455 (August 2006).

24. Timothy Guinnane, Ron Harris, Naomi R. Lamoreaux and Jean-Laurent Rosenthal, 'Putting the Corporation in its Place', NBER Working Paper 13109 (May 2007); Aldo Musacchio, *Experiments in Financial Democracy: Corporate Governance and Financial Development in Brazil, 1882–1950* (Cambridge, 2009).

25. David Collison, Stuart Cross, John Ferguson, David Power and Lorna Stevenson, 'Legal Determinants of External Finance Revisited: The Inverse Relationship between Investor Protection and Societal Well-Being', *Journal of Business Ethics*, 108 (2012), pp. 393–410.

26. Charles Dickens, *Bleak House* (1852–3), ch. 1.

27. Michael Slater, *Dickens: A Life Defined by Writing* (New Haven, 2009), esp. pp. 340–58.

28. Richard Danzig, 'Hadley v. Baxendale: A Study in the Industrialization of the Law', *Journal of Legal Studies*, 4, 2 (June 1975), pp. 267f.

29. Rande W. Kostal, *Law and English Railway Capitalism, 1825–1875* (Oxford, 1994).

30. Danzig, 'Hadley v. Baxendale', p. 277.

31. Ibid., p. 252n.

32. Ibid., p. 254.

33. *Kleinwort Benson* v. *Lincoln City Council* [1999] 2 AC 349, Lord Goff at pp. 377ff.

34. Philip K. Howard, 'It's Time to Clean House', *Atlantic Monthly*, 14 March 2012.

35. Idem, 'Results-Based Regulation: A Blueprint for Starting Over', *Common Good*, 2 December 2011: http://www.commongood.org/blog/entry/philip-k.-howard-on-the-need-for-results-based-regulation.

36. Calculated from data in Ida A. Brudnick, 'Congressional Salaries and Allowances', Congressional Research Service report, 4 January 2011; Office of Management and Budget, *Fiscal Year 2013 Budget of the U.S. Government* (Washington, DC, 2010); the 2013 Federal Judicial Budget. See also Susan Dudley and Melinda Warren, 'Fiscal Stalemate Reflected in Regulators' Budget: An Analysis of the U.S. Budget for Fiscal Years 2011 and 2012', Regulators' Budget Report 33, 11 May 2011.

37. 2011 actual expenditure listed in Center for Responsive Politics Report: http://www.opensecrets.org/lobby/index.php.

38. Nicole V. Crain and W. Mark Crain, 'The Impact of Regulatory Costs on Small Firms', Small Business Administration, Office of Advocacy (September 2010).

39. Lawrence J. McQuillan, Hovannes Abramyan and Anthony P. Archie, *Jackpot Justice: The True Cost of America's Tort System* (San Francisco, 2007), p. xii.

40. Lawrence J. McQuillan and Hovannes Abramyan, *U.S. Tort Liability Index: 2010 Report* (San Francisco, 2010), p. 18. Cf. Towers Perrin, *2009 Update on U.S. Tort Cost Trends* (n.p., 2009).

41. Lawrence Chimerine and Ross Eisenbrey, 'The Frivolous Case for Tort Law Change: Opponents of the Legal System Exaggerate its Costs, Ignore its Benefits', Economic Policy Institute Briefing Paper (May 2005).

42. David Kennedy and Joseph Stiglitz, *Law and Economics with Chinese Characteristics: Institutions for Promoting Development in the Twenty-First Century* (forthcoming).

43. Michael E. Porter, Mercedes Delgado, Christian Ketels and Scott Stern, 'Moving to a New Global Competitiveness Index', in World Economic Forum, *Global Competitiveness Report, 2008–2009* (Geneva, 2009).

44. Michael E. Porter and Jan W. Rivkin, 'The Looming Challenge to U.S. Competitiveness', *Harvard Business Review* (March 2012), and the same authors' 'Choosing the United States', ibid.

45. World Economic Forum, *Global Competitiveness Report, 2011–2012* (Geneva, 2011).

46. Heritage Foundation, *Index of Economic Freedom 2011* (Washington, DC, 2011): http://www.heritage.org/index/ranking.

47. International Finance Corporation, *Doing Business 2011* (Washington, DC, 2011).

48. World Justice Project, Rule of Law Index 2011 (Washington, DC, 2011).

49. World Bank, Worldwide Governance Index: www.gov indicators.org.

50. International Financial Corporation, Doing Business data-set: http://www.doingbusiness.org/.

51. Stephan Haggard and Lydia Tiede, 'The Rule of Law and Economic Growth: Where Are We?', *World Development*, 39, 5 (2011), pp. 673–85.

52. For an excellent survey, see Michael Trebilcock and Jing Leng, 'The Role of Formal Contract Law and Enforcement in Economic Development', *Virginia Law Review*, 92 (2006), pp. 1517–80, esp. pp. 1554–75.

53. Daron Acemoglu and James A. Robinson, *Why Nations Fail: The Origins of Power, Prosperity, and Poverty* (New York, 2012), pp. 445f.

54. Donald C. Clarke, 'Power and Politics in the Chinese Court System: The Enforcement of Civil Judgments', *Columbia Journal of Asian Law*, 10, 1 (1996), pp. 1–125.

55. See He Weifang, *In the Name of Justice*, passim.

56. Ethan Michelson and Sida Lui, 'What Do Chinese Lawyers Want? Political Values and Legal Practice', in Cheng Li (ed.), *China's Emerging Middle Class: Beyond Economic Transformation* (Washington, DC, 2010), pp. 310f., 316, 320, 328f.

57. Lulu Chen, 'Mainland's Last Chance to Reform', *South China Morning Post*, 3 June 2012.

58. He Weifang, 'Constitutionalism as a Global Trend and its Impact on China (2004)', in idem, *In the Name of Justice*.

59. Mancur Olson, *The Rise and Decline of Nations: Economic Growth, Stagflation and Social Rigidities* (New Haven/London, 1982).

60. R. Eric Petersen, 'Representatives and Senators: Trends in Member Characteristics since 1945', Congressional

Research Service, 17 February 2012; Jennifer E. Manning, 'Membership of the 112th Congress: A Profile', Congressional Research Service, 1 March 2011; Edmund Tetteh, 'Election Statistics: UK 1918–2007', House of Commons Library Research Paper 08/12, 1 February 2008.

Chapter 4: Civil and Uncivil Societies

1. Alexis de Tocqueville, *Democracy in America*, trans. Harvey C. Mansfield and Delba Winthrop (Chicago, 2000), book I, part 2, ch. 4.
2. Ibid., book II, part 2, ch. 5.
3. Ibid.
4. Marvin Olasky, *The Tragedy of American Compassion* (Washington, DC, 1992).
5. Edward C. Banfield, *The Moral Basis of a Backward Society* (Glencoe, IL, 1958).
6. Robert D. Putnam, *Bowling Alone: The Collapse and Revival of American Community* (New York, 2000).
7. Theda Skocpol, *Diminished Democracy: From Membership to Management in American Life* (Norman, OK, 2003).
8. Charles Murray, *Coming Apart: The State of White America, 1960–2010* (New York, 2012).
9. Peter Hall, 'Social Capital in Britain', *British Journal of Politics*, 29 (1999), p. 419.
10. José Harris, 'Society and the State in Twentieth Century Britain', in F. M. L. Thompson (ed.), *The Cambridge Social*

History of Britain 1750–1950, vol. III: *Social Agencies and Institutions* (Oxford, 1990), p. 68.

11. Robert Humphreys, *Poor Relief and Charity, 1869–1945* (London, 2001), tables 2.7, 3.2, 4.1 and 4.2, pp. 55, 68, 105, 109.

12. Jane Lewis, *The Voluntary Sector, the State, and Social Work in Britain: The Charity Organisation Society and the Family Welfare Association since 1869* (London, 1995).

13. Peter A. Hall, 'Social Capital in Britain', *British Journal of Political Science*, 29 (1999), pp. 421f.

14. Compare 'Friendly Societies', *British Medical Journal*, 25 December 1909, with Register of Friendly Societies, *Report of the Chief Registrar, 2000–2001* (London, 2001).

15. P. H. J. H. Gosden, *Self-Help: Voluntary Associations in the Nineteenth Century* (Leeds, 1973), tables 3.1 and 4.5, pp. 42, 104.

16. Evan Schofer and Marion Fourcade-Gourinchas, 'The Structural Contexts of Civic Engagement: Voluntary Association Membership in Comparative Perspective', *American Sociological Review*, 66 (December 2001), p. 808.

17. National Council for Voluntary Organizations, *Participation: Trends, Facts and Figures* (March 2011), p. 18.

18. Edd Cowley, Tom McKenzie, Cathy Pharoah and Sarah Smith, 'The New State of Donation: Three Decades of Household Giving to Charity, 1978–2008', Centre for Market and Public Organisation, University of Bristol (February 2011).

19. Robert Rutherfoord, *Community Action in England: A Report on the 2009–10 Citizenship Survey* (December 2011); idem,

Community Spirit in England: A Report on the 2009–10 Citizenship Survey (December 2011).

20. Eric Schmidt and Jared Cohen, 'The Digital Disruption: Connectivity and the Diffusion of Power', *Foreign Affairs* (November/December, 2010).

21. Nicole B. Ellison, Charles Steinfield and Cliff Lampe, 'The Benefits of Facebook "Friends": Social Capital and College Students' Use of Online Social Network Sites', *Journal of Computer-Mediated Communication*, 12, 4 (2007): http://jcmc.indiana.edu/vol12/issue4/ellison.html. See also Nicole B. Ellison, Charles Steinfield and Cliff Lampe, 'Connection Strategies: Social Capital Implications of Facebook-Enabled Communication Practices', *New Media Society*, 13, 6 (2011), pp. 873–92.

22. Tocqueville, *Democracy in America*, book II, part 4, ch. 6.

23. Ibid., part 2, ch. 5.

24. Peter H. Lindert, 'Voice and Growth: Was Churchill Right?', *Journal of Economic History*, 63, 2 (June 2003), pp. 315–50; idem, 'Why the Welfare State Looks Like a Free Lunch', NBER Working Paper 9869 (July 2003). See also Sun Go and Peter H. Lindert, 'The Curious Dawn of American Public Schools', NBER Working Paper 13335 (August 2007).

25. Paul Collier, 'Private v State: Here's How to Bridge the Educational Divide', *Independent*, 14 January 2010.

26. 'The Horse before the Cart', *Economist*, 17 September 2011.

27. 'Education Reform: Back to School', *Economist*, 9 September 2011.

28. Mogens Kamp Justesen, 'Learning from Europe: Parental Empowerment in the Dutch and Danish Education Systems', Adam Smith Institute (2002).

29. Results for 2010–11 at http://www.successacademies.org/page.cfm?p=11.

30. 'The Ties that Bind', *Economist*, 28 March 2012.

31. James Tooley, *The Beautiful Tree: A Personal Journey into How the World's Poorest People are Educating Themselves* (Washington, DC, 2009).

32. Martin West and Ludger Woessmann, '"Every Catholic in a Catholic School": Historical Resistance to State Schooling, Contemporary School Competition, and Student Achievement across Countries', *Economic Journal*, 120, 546 (2010), pp. 229–55.

33. Toby Helm and Julian Coman, 'Rowan Williams Pours Scorn on David Cameron's "Big Society"', *Guardian*, 24 June 2012.

34. 'Martin Sime Addresses the Big Society in Scotland Conference', 28 October 2011: http://www.scvo.org.uk/scvo-news/martin-sime-addresses-the-big-society-in-scotland-conference/.

Conclusion

1. Robert C. Allen, Jean-Pascal Bassino, Debin Ma, Christine Moll-Murata and Jan Luiten van Zanden, 'Wages, Prices, and Living Standards in China, 1739–1925: In Comparison

with Europe, Japan, and India', *Economic History Review*, 64 (2011), table 3, p. 36.

2. Orley C. Ashenfelter, 'Comparing Real Wages', NBER Working Paper 18006 (April 2012).

3. Ron Unz, 'Race, IQ and Wealth', *American Conservative* (August 2012), a devastating critique of Richard Lynn and Tatu Vanhanen, *IQ and the Wealth of Nations* (Westport, CT, 2002).

4. Calculated from Emmanuel Saez's file TabFig2010.xls, figure A1, available at http://emlab.berkeley.edu/users/saez/.

5. Ibid., data-Fig A1, available at http://emlab.berkeley.edu/users/saez/.

6. McKinsey Global Institute, *Urban World: Cities and the Rise of the Consuming Class* (June 2012), p. 20. See also McKinsey Global Institute, *India's Urban Awakening: Building Inclusive Cities, Sustaining Economic Growth* (April 2010).

7. Geoffrey West, 'Why Cities Keep Growing, Corporations and People Always Die, and Life Gets Faster', *Edge*, 17 July 2011. See also West's dazzling TED lecture: http://www.ted.com/talks/geoffrey_west_the_surprising_math_of_cities_and_corporations.html.

8. Based on data in David Cohen, 'Earth's Natural Wealth: An Audit', *New Scientist*, 23 May 2007, fossil-fuel statistics from BP and market prices in mid-2011.

9. Michael Milken, 'Where's Sputnik? Summoning the Will to Create the Next American Century', *Milken Institute Review*, 2nd Quarter (2011), pp. 1–20.

10. Ernst & Young, *The World is Bumpy: Globalization and New Strategies for Growth* (2012), figure 4, p. 8.

11. Steven Pinker, *The Better Angels of our Nature: The Decline of Violence and its Psychological Roots* (New York, 2011).

12. Andrew Odlyzko, 'Crushing National Debts, Economic Revolutions, and Extraordinary Popular Delusions', University of Minnesota Working Paper (2012).

13. Carmen M. Reinhart, Vincent R. Reinhart and Kenneth S. Rogoff, 'Debt Overhangs: Past and Present', NBER Working Paper 18015 (April 2012).

14. Paul Krugman, 'Money for Nothing', *New York Times*, 26 July 2012.

15. Peter Thiel, 'Swift Blind Horseman', *National Review*, 3 October 2011.

16. Peter Turchin, 'Dynamics of Political Instability in the United States, 1780–2010', *Journal of Peace Research*.

17. Remarks by the President at a Campaign Event in Roanoke, Virginia, 13 July 2012: http://www.whitehouse.gov/the-press-office/2012/07/13/remarks-president-campaign-event-roanoke-virginia.

Acknowledgements

This book began life as the BBC Radio 4 Reith Lectures 2012, so I must begin by thanking Gwyneth Williams, who invited me to give the lectures, Hugh Levinson, who edited them, Jane Beresford, who produced them, and Sue Lawley, who introduced them. Previous Reith lecturers constitute some of the hardest acts in the world to follow. The BBC team made the task less intimidating and more fun than I had anticipated.

Thanks are also due to Leeann Saw, who acted as my research assistant for this project, Simon Winder and Ann Godoff, my editors in, respectively, London and New York, and Andrew Wylie, my agent.

A number of expert friends generously read and commented on drafts of the lectures or chapters. In particular, I would like to thank Charles Béar, Harold Carter, Douglas Flint and Paul Tucker. Thanks are also due to my colleagues at Greenmantle: Pierpaolo Barbieri, Joshua Lachter, Hassan Malik and Jason Rockett, who contributed directly and indirectly to the completion of the manuscript.

Those academics who have written on the subject of institutions and development are acknowledged in the text and notes. I cannot unfortunately do the same for all the audience members who asked insightful questions after I delivered the lectures, though I am grateful to them, too. I can and do thank the four institutions that hosted the lectures: the London School of Economics, the New York Historical Society, Gresham College and the Royal Society of Edinburgh.

Finally, these lectures were devised, written, delivered and turned into a book during the first seven months of my youngest son's life. This book is dedicated to him.

ALSO AVAILABLE

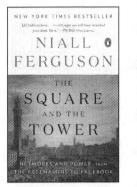 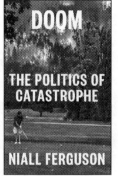 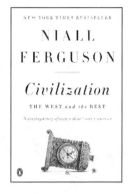

DOOM
The Politics of Catastrophe

THE SQUARE AND THE TOWER
Networks and Power, from the Freemasons to Facebook

KISSINGER
1923-1968: The Idealist

THE ASCENT OF MONEY
A Financial History of the World

CIVILIZATION
The West and the Rest

HIGH FINANCIER
The Lives and Time of Siegmund Warburg

THE WAR OF THE WORLD
Twentieth-Century Conflict and the Descent of the West

COLOSSUS
The Rise and Fall of the American Empire

THE HOUSE OF ROTHSCHILD
Volume 1: Money's Prophets: 1798-1848
Volume 2: The World's Banker: 1849-1999

⊞ PENGUIN PRESS   Ⓟ PENGUIN BOOKS

Ready to find your next great read? Let us help. Visit prh.com/nextread